BRAIN GA

MW00861306

PUZZLES AND QUIZZES

UNAUTHORIZED AND UNOFFICIAL

Facts and Info about Taylor Swift

Publications International, Ltd.

Contributing writers: Elsa Harbison and Arie Kaplan

Images from Shutterstock.com

Louis Weber, CEO
Publications International, Ltd.
8140 Lehigh Avenue
Morton Grove, IL 60053

ISBN: 978-1-63938-639-0

Manufactured in China.

8 7 6 5 4 3 2 1

Let's get social!
@Publications_International
@PublicationsInternational
@BrainGames.TM
www.pilbooks.com

Puzzles for Swifties!

Can I ask you a question? Are you a mastermind? Put your Swiftie knowledge to the test with **Brain Games® Puzzles and Quizzes: Facts and Info about** Taylor Swift! This collection contains more than 85 puzzles, including word searches, matching puzzles, crosswords, picture puzzles, and word scrambles. Solve clues about albums and tours, hunt for musical influences, unscramble track titles, guess songs based on pictures, and much more. If you need a hint, puzzle answers are found at the back of the book. Challenge your friends and yourself with fun trivia quizzes! Fifteen trivia quizzes appear throughout the book, with questions on right-hand pages and answers on the following left-hand pages. Like any good game, this one keeps you guessing.

Anti-Hero

The *Anti-Hero* music video from Swift's *Midnights* was written and directed by Swift herself. The video follows three incarnations of Swift, each illustrating a different insecurity of hers. The vintage set includes fun-to-find Easter Eggs like the rotary phone from the *We Are Never Ever Getting Back Together* music video, the blue guitar used during the Speak Now tour, and heart-shaped sunglasses worn in the *22* music video. Can you find four changes between these two photographs?

Answers on page 146.

TRIVIA

1. When Taylor was growing up, she was raised on what type of farm?

    A. Dairy farm
    C. Apiculture farm
    B. Christmas tree farm
    D. Soybean farm

2. What did Taylor write when she was 12 years old?

    A. Novel
    C. Poem
    B. Commercial jingle
    D. Movie script

3. Which relative of Taylor's was an opera singer?

    A. Grandfather
    C. Great-grandfather
    B. Great-aunt
    D. Grandmother

4. Which singer was one of Taylor's early inspirations?

    A. Alicia Keys
    C. LeAnn Rimes
    B. Sheryl Crow
    D. Selena Gomez

5. When Taylor was in the fourth grade, she won a poetry competition for a poem called...

    A. "Have You Seen Him?"
    C. "I Don't Know What to Do"
    B. "Pounce"
    D. "Monster in My Closet"

1. B. Taylor grew up on a Christmas tree farm. There, she enjoyed the wide open spaces and she rode horses. In fact, her experiences on this farm inspired her to write the 2019 song "Christmas Tree Farm."

2. A. At just 12 years old, Taylor spent a summer writing a 350-page novel. Even then, the urge to write and create was in Taylor's heart. These days, she writes songs, not novels. But she hasn't ruled out the possibility of writing her own autobiography at some point in the future.

3. D. Taylor's maternal grandmother Marjorie Finlay was an opera singer who sang with the Puerto Rico Symphony Orchestra. Taylor has said that when she was younger, her grandmother was a huge inspiration. More recently, Taylor included recordings of her grandmother singing as backing vocals in the song "marjorie."

4. C. LeAnn Rimes was one of Taylor's earliest musical heroes. In fact, Taylor was only six years old when she got her first LeAnn Rimes CD.

5. D. In the fourth grade, Taylor won a national poetry competition with her poem, "Monster in My Closet." The poem starts out with the following lines: There's a monster in my closet and I don't know what to do! Have you ever seen him? Has he ever pounced on you?

Addagram

In addition to being scrambled, each phrase below is missing the same letter. Discover the missing letter, then unscramble the words. When you do, you'll reveal 3 singles from Taylor Swift's self-titled debut album.

PRY A MODERATING SORT

CONTRITE BURP

DOODLES VANISH

Matching

Match each Taylor Swift song to the musician it features.

1. "Snow on the Beach"
2. "Everything Has Changed"
3. "Fortnight"
4. "exile"
5. "Breathe"
6. "ME!"

A. Bon Iver
B. Brendon Urie
C. Ed Sheeran
D. Colbie Caillat
E. Lana Del Rey
F. Post Malone

Answers on page 146.

reputation

ACROSS

1. This song was inspired by the TV series *Game of Thrones*
7. When reputation dies, you can feel ____
8. Upon its release, Taylor described *reputation* as her "most ____ album"
10. Title of track 8
14. What famous 1960s film is referenced in "Getaway Car"?
16. Streaming service that hosted the concert film of the Reputation Stadium Tour
17. Co-writer of "This Is Why We Can't Have Nice Things"
21. Celebrity featured in the *Look What You Made Me Do* and *You Need to Calm Down* music videos
23. Why can't Taylor be reached? 'Cause ____
25. Name of child whose voice is sampled at the beginning of "Gorgeous"
28. If there is no explanation, what is there?
29. Title of track 7

DOWN

2. Swift released "I Don't Wanna Live Forever" with ZAYN for what movie?
3. Rapper, co-writer, and featured artist on "End Game"
4. The name of the era of Swift's dyed blonde hair, circa *reputation*
5. Number of bonus tracks on the album
6. *reputation* was Swift's ____ album produced under Big Machine Records
9. *reputation* release month
11. Title of track 14
12. Celebrity who cameos in the concert version of "Look What You Made Me Do"
13. Associated album color
15. She fell ____
18. Swift's pseudonym under which she wrote "This Is What You Came For" for Calvin Harris
19. Number of songs on the album
20. In what music video was "King of My Heart" first teased?
22. Song in which Swift's bleached hair is referenced
23. *reputation* is which album in her discography?
24. Song in which a "dive bar" is mentioned
26. City featured in the Reputation Stadium Tour concert film
27. Associated album animal

Name the Songs

Solve these shrouded mysteries! Guess each Taylor Swift song based on the pictures shown.

1.

2.

3.

Answers on page 146.

Taylor Swift Scramble

Can you make sense of something crazy? Unscramble each phrase below to reveal a song from Taylor Swift's self-titled debut album.

1. DISSOLVE A HOUND

2. LOUSY CODA

3. GOO RUNS

4. MR. TWIG CAM

5. PUNCTURE ORBIT

6. SPUR A TRIGONOMETRY AD

7. MY MOSSY GYM HARMONY

8. A PILCHARD'S TOWLINE

9. ED LIGHTS A METEORITE WITH

10. SHOUTED TIE

11. ITS FAULTY BEAU

12. CRAFTED A HERPETOLOGY

Answers on page 146.

One-Word Song Titles

Every Taylor Swift song title listed is contained within the group of letters. Titles can be found in a straight line horizontally, vertically, or diagonally. They may be read either forward or backward.

AFTERGLOW	HOAX
BABE	INVISIBLE
CARDIGAN	IVY
CLEAN	LOVER
DAYLIGHT	MAROON
EPIPHANY	MASTERMIND
EVERMORE	MEAN
FIFTEEN	PEACE
FORTNIGHT	SEVEN
GLITCH	STYLE
HAPPINESS	WILLOW

```
P E A C T S F E G I L Y A D P I
R N N A H H S Y P M A R O E C M
L I A R G V V E P I P H A N Y R
O P E D I I A C N S P C Y O A E
V P L I L Y T S I I E H H O A T
E A C G Y N E V E S P V A R F S
R H F C A R D I G A N P E A T A
N D I W D N I M R E T S A M E M
N H F I T H G I N T R O F H R I
F E T L O M R E V E V M T A G N
L O E L S E R O M R E V E E L V
O F R T E L Y T S H O A R L D I
V T H T F B P H C T I L G C B S
E M O O N I N V I S I B L E A I
M E A N A I F V I L G C O S B B
B A B W V X G W O L L I W X E B
```

Find the Cats

We're playing hide-and-seek. Can you find doppelgangers of Taylor Swift's 3 cats—Meredith Grey, Olivia Benson, and Benjamin Button—hidden in the picture?

Answers on page 147.

TRIVIA

1. Taylor's first job was knocking the ____ out of Christmas trees on her family's farm.

    A. Hornet nests   C. Spiderwebs

    B. Praying mantis pods   D. Beehives

2. Which cat is draped around Taylor's shoulders in her iconic *TIME Magazine* Person of the Year shot?

    A. Phoebe Buffay   C. Olivia Benson

    B. Meredith Grey   D. Benjamin Button

3. Before Taylor's mother, Andrea, was a homemaker, she was a(n) _____.

    A. Dentist   C. Marketing executive

    B. Lawyer   D. Accountant

4. When Taylor was a child, her father Scott worked as a ____.

    A. Stockbroker   C. Doctor

    B. Talent agent   D. Photographer

5. When Taylor was 14, she and her family moved to ____.

    A. Knoxville   C. Franklin

    B. Memphis   D. Hendersonville

Answers on following page.

1. B. When Taylor was a child, she had a really unusual job: to knock praying mantis pods out of Christmas trees. That way, they wouldn't hatch in people's homes when they took the trees with them for the holidays.

2. D. Taylor's blue-eyed ragdoll cat Benjamin Button is featured in her iconic TIME Magazine Person of the Year cover, shot by Inez and Vinoodh. Benjamin Button also made an appearance during writer Sam Lansky's interview with Taylor for TIME.

3. C. Andrea was a marketing executive. She's been a staunch supporter of Taylor's career since day one, and Taylor often consults her mother for advice on any major decision she's about to make.

4. A. Scott was a stockbroker when Taylor was growing up. He worked for Merrill Lynch. In fact, one of Scott's clients sold him the Christmas tree farm where Taylor was raised.

5. D. When Taylor was in middle school, her parents moved the family to Hendersonville, Tennessee. That way, Taylor could be closer to Nashville, where she would pursue her musical dreams!

Emoji Songs

We're searching for a sign. Based on the emojis, guess each Taylor Swift song.

1.

2.

3.

4.

5.

reputation scramble

Unscramble each phrase below to reveal a song from Taylor Swift's *reputation* album.

1. ANYWAY, DEERS

2. IS STOOGE

3. A CAD SHREDDING WITHOUT INN

4. RACEWAY TAG

5. CHASTENING EACH WHINY HIVE TWISTS

6. FRAYED RIOT

7. MAD GENE

8. ATTACH WILLOWY AUNT

9. LACED TIE

10. A HOOKY MODULATED MEOW

11. FORAGE HYMN KIT

12. GOOSE RUG

Answers on page 147.

Word Fill-In

We've got a blank space, baby. Use each of the words given to complete this clueless crossword grid. The puzzle has only one solution.

3 letters

DAY
RED

4 letters

CALM
DOWN
PLAY

5 letters

LYRIC
REMIX
STAGE
VAULT
VINYL

6 letters

GUITAR
SINGLE

7 letters

PERFORM

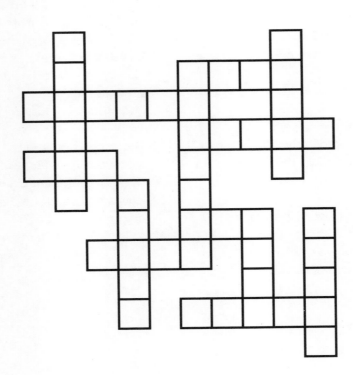

Midnights

ACROSS

1. On what platform did Taylor announce the album's track titles?
3. This TV show inspired the title of "Lavender Haze"
7. What song inspired the friendship bracelet movement?
9. This fish was featured in the *Lavender Haze* music video
10. Highly-anticipated collaborator on "Snow on the Beach"
14. This track was the closing song in the Eras Tour setlist
15. *Midnights* won the Grammy for Best Pop ____
17. How many Grammy Awards was *Midnights* nominated for?
19. Aaron Dessner co-wrote this *3am* track
21. The *Bejeweled* music video had several Easter Eggs for this re-record
24. Title of track 9
26. Swift was featured in this film which opened weeks before the album's release
27. Title of *3am* track 4
28. Number of Billboard 100 spots the album earned in its first week
29. What time is included in the title of the extended version of the album?

DOWN

2. Number of tracks on the original version of the album
3. Title of track 2
4. *Til ____ Edition*
5. This actress co-wrote "Lavender Haze"
6. Co-writer of "Sweet Nothing"
8. Swift announced *Midnights* at the MTV Video ____
11. Swift won a record-breaking fourth ____ Grammy for *Midnights*
12. Most-streamed song on the album since its release
13. Number of cities around the world Swift placed billboards with lyrics from the album leading up to its release
16. Besides "Anti-Hero," this song also had an acoustic version and several remixes
17. The album was inspired by "13 ____ nights" of Taylor's life
18. This actress played the wicked stepmom in the *Bejeweled* video
19. Director of the *Anti-Hero* music video
20. How many songs on the album include colors in their titles?
22. Artist featured on the remix of "Karma"
23. *Midnights* is which album in her discography?
25. "Midnights ____ with Me"

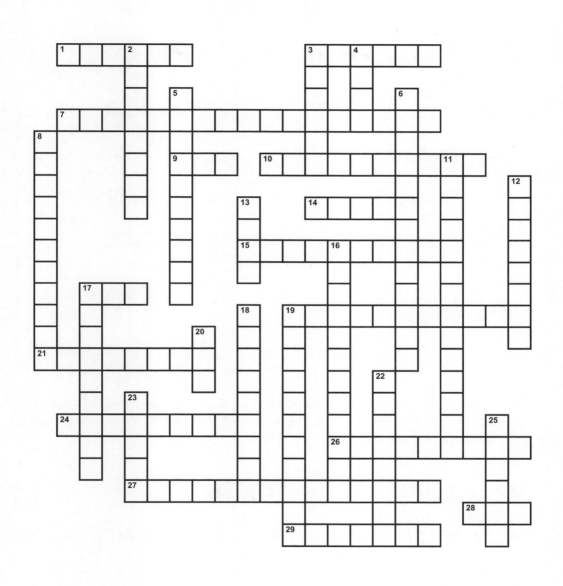

Answers on page 147.

21

Matching

Match each film to the year in which Taylor Swift appeared in it.

1. *Cats*   A. 2010

2. *Amsterdam*   B. 2014

3. *Valentine's Day*   C. 2019

4. *The Giver*   D. 2022

Addagram

Are you a mastermind? In addition to being scrambled, each phrase below is missing the same letter. Discover the missing letter, then unscramble the words. When you do, you'll reveal 4 singles from Taylor Swift's *Fearless* album.

WHOSE HEIR   FIN FEE

VERY SOLO   WHY BEGUILE MOON

Answers on pages 147–148.

ERAS Opening Acts

Every opening act from Taylor Swift's Eras Tour listed is contained within the group of letters. Names can be found in a straight line horizontally, vertically, or diagonally. They may be read either forward or backward.

BEABADOOBEE

GAYLE

GIRL IN RED

GRACIE (Abrams)

HAIM

LOUTA

MUNA

OWENN

PARAMORE

PHOEBE (Bridgers)

SABRINA (Carpenter)

```
P O G I R L I N R G E
H P M E P O G A R E B
O G E M N U M A B H M
E I R I R T C O Y I O
M R O N L A O A A L W
U L M G L D P H R D E
N I A S A B R I N A N
A N R B G O W E N N D
G R A C I E I R B A S
U E P H O E B E H A I
B D B E A B A D O O S
```

Love Story

Filmed at Castle Gwynn in Tennessee, the swoon-worthy *Love Story* music video from Swift's second album, *Fearless,* is a longtime fan favorite. The video was released in 2009, about seven months after the album, and has garnered hundreds of millions of views on YouTube.

TRIVIA

1. Taylor met her friend Hayley Williams when they were both competing for the _____ Grammy in 2008.

   A. Songwriter of the Year   **C.** Best New Artist

   B. Best New Album   **D.** Record of the Year

2. According to *People Magazine*, once when Taylor Swift and Hayley Williams attended a wedding together, they ditched the reception and hung out at...

   A. The Cheesecake Factory   **C.** Applebee's

   B. Chili's   **D.** Dave & Buster's

3. Taylor wrote a song which appeared on the soundtrack of the 2009 film *Hannah Montana: The Movie*. Which song was it?

   A. "Hoedown Throwdown"   **C.** "The Good Life"

   B. "Spotlight"   **D.** "You'll Always Find Your Way Back Home"

4. As a child, Taylor appeared in musicals produced by _____.

   A. People's Light   **C.** Centre Stage

   B. Berks County Youth Theatre   **D.** Pennsylvania Youth Theatre

5. Who was Taylor named after?

Answers on following page.

1. **C.** Taylor and Hayley were competing for the Best New Artist Award at the Grammys in 2008. And if the name "Hayley Williams" sounds familiar, it's because she's the lead vocalist for the rock group Paramore.

2. **A.** They went to the Cheesecake Factory. Taylor and Hayley have been good friends ever since 2008, and they've been there for each other on many occasions. Hayley has said that once when she was going through a difficult period, Taylor called her and told her jokes to cheer her up.

3. **D.** Taylor co-wrote the song "You'll Always Find Your Way Back Home" with fellow tunesmith Martin Johnson for the 2009 film. Taylor also made a cameo in *Hannah Montana: The Movie*. The following year, Taylor and Martin worked together on the *Speak Now* cut of the song "If This Was a Movie."

4. **B.** Around the time she moved to Wyomissing, Pennsylvania, Taylor began appearing in musicals produced by Berks County Youth Theatre. While a member of their theater academy, Taylor realized she liked singing more than acting and entered karaoke contests weekly.

5. Taylor was named after James Taylor, one of her parents' favorite artists. She performed with her namesake James Taylor at Madison Square Garden in 2011. Taylor also mentioned James Taylor in the lyrics to her song "Begin Again."

Name the Songs

Think we can solve them? Guess each Taylor Swift song based on the pictures shown.

1.

2.

 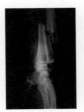  

3.

Answers on page 148.

FEARLESS SCRAMBLE

Unscramble each phrase below to reveal a song from the *Fearless (Taylor's Version)* album.

1. BEGONE WILY MOUTH

2. OVERTLY SO

3. SALES REF

4. EITHER SHOW

5. YOUR ROSY TONER

6. FREEWAYS & VALOR

7. WEAVED OILY YOUTH

8. TEE HYPHENS

9. ABET HER

10. NET FIFE

11. THEY BASTED

12. FENCER PET FIRMLY

13. YOUR MALE VOLE

Answers on page 148.

ERAS TOUR QUIZ

Below are the designers of Taylor Swift's Eras Tour costumes. The only thing is, they've lost all instances of A, E, I, O, U, and Y. Can you figure out the missing vowels and name each designer in the list below?

1. V_RS_C_

2. CHR_ST__N L__B__T_N

3. R_B_RT_ C_V_LL_

4. _TR_

5. _SH_SH

6. N_C_L_ + F_L_C__

7. _LB_RT_ F_RR_TT_

8. J_SS_C_ J_N_S

9. Z_H__R M_R_D

10. _SC_R D_ L_ R_NT_

evermore

ACROSS

1. "champagne problems" is about a ____
4. The beginning of the *willow* music video begins right where the ____ music video ended
7. Which song was the last single to be released off of the album?
9. "'tis the damn season" and ____ are parallel songs, telling two sides of a love story
10. How many "willow" remixes have been released?
12. Heart-wrenching song describing a partner's cruel indifference
14. Taylor's hairstyle on the album cover, now a symbol of the era
15. In what song does Swift mention "Olive Garden"?
18. Swift just couldn't ____ after *folklore*, resulting in this new album just months later
21. Jack Antonoff's favorite song on the *evermore* album
24. Number of tracks on the original version of the album
25. Featured group on "no body, no crime"
26. Associated album season
27. Number of bonus tracks on the deluxe version
28. Taeok Lee, Taylor's opposite in the *willow* music video, toured with her as a background dancer for the ____ tour
29. Swift's ____ can be heard through her operatic vocals in "marjorie"

DOWN

1. *evermore*'s sister album
2. Title of track 14
3. Featured group on "coney island"
4. William Bowery co-wrote what song about a tragic young love story?
5. The *willow* music video was Swift's ____ self-directed music video
6. Song that Swift recorded just one week before the album's release
8. *evermore* release month
11. Frontman of Mumford & Sons who provides backing vocals on "cowboy like me"
13. Title of track 12
16. *evermore* is which album in Taylor's discography?
17. Second bonus track off of the album, opposite "right where you left me"
19. This TV/podcast genre inspired "no body, no crime" and is one of Swift's longtime favorites
20. The sum of the number of tracks on *folklore* and *evermore*, equal to the age Swift was turning around *evermore*'s release
22. Collaborator and featured artist on the track "evermore"
23. "dorothea" was the ____ track Taylor wrote for the album

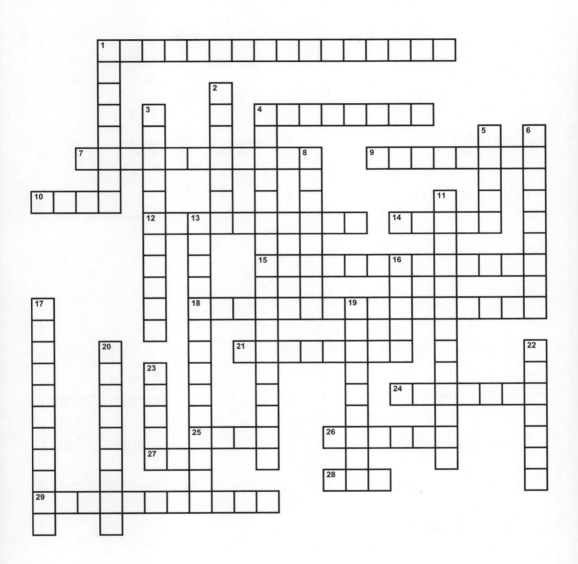

Answers on page 148.

Addagram

In addition to being scrambled, each word or phrase below is missing the same letter. Discover the missing letter, then unscramble the words. When you do, you'll reveal 4 London locales mentioned in Taylor Swift's "London Boy" song.

NEWEST

THIS CHORE

CEMENT KARMA

NO BETTERS

Matching

Match each Taylor Swift song to the co-writer.

1. "Picture to Burn"

2. "Labyrinth"

3. "Treacherous"

4. "cardigan"

5. "You Need to Calm Down"

6. "Clean"

A. Aaron Dessner

B. Imogen Heap

C. Jack Antonoff

D. Liz Rose

E. Joel Little

F. Dan Wilson

Answers on page 149.

Names in Titles

Every name in a Taylor Swift song title listed is contained within the group of letters. Names can be found in a straight line horizontally, vertically, or diagonally. They may be read either forward or backward.

AUGUST   EMMA   MARY

BETTY   GRACE   RONAN

CLARA   IVY   STEPHEN

CORNELIA   JOHN   TIM MCGRAW

DOROTHEA   MARJORIE

```
C S O A A U G U S T P C
U V M M E C O R N E L U
H M R R H W M A C Y M A
E O A G T Y N A E V B R
T M J M O O R D M I S A
I J W A R G C M M I T L
M O V R O A U G U C E C
M H I J D P T T E B P R
C N C O R N E L I A H O
G M A R G M A R Y J E N
R N N I R O J R A M N A
L C B E T T Y H P E T S
```

Answers on page 149.

Word Fill-In

Use each of the words and names given to complete this clueless crossword grid. The puzzle has only one solution.

3 letters

ACT
ERA
NOW
OWN
SET

4 letters

STAY
TOUR

5 letters

AWARD
SPEAK

6 letters

WRITER

7 letters

BREATHE
COUNTRY

8 letters

EVERMORE
FEARLESS

Answers on page 149.

TRIVIA

1. Which Rihanna song did Taylor write?

   A. "Umbrella"

   B. "Take a Bow"

   C. "This Is What You Came For"

   D. "Diamonds"

2. Taylor was the first non-comedian *Saturday Night Live* host in history to write their own...

   A. Weekend Update jokes

   B. Script for a digital short

   C. Cold open sketch

   D. Monologue

3. Taylor first appeared on *Saturday Night Live* in the year...

   A. 2009

   B. 2015

   C. 2017

   D. 2021

4. In 2021, Taylor appeared in a hilarious *SNL* digital short called...

   A. "Roast"

   B. "The Original Princes of Comedy"

   C. "Three Sad Virgins"

   D. "Hanxiety"

5. On Valentine's Day 2024, an actor who's famous for playing a Marvel superhero told *Variety* that he was a Taylor Swift fan. Who is the superhero Swiftie?

   A. Chris Hemsworth

   B. Simu Liu

   C. Paul Rudd

   D. Anthony Mackie

Answers on following page.

1. **C.** Taylor wrote "This Is What You Came For" for Rihanna and Calvin Harris. In the official credits, the songwriter is listed as "Nils Sjoberg," a pseudonym for Taylor Swift!

2. **D.** Yup, Taylor was the first non-comedian SNL host to write their own monologue. Since Taylor is a songwriter, her monologue consisted of a hilarious tune called "Monologue Song (La La La)." In the song, she sang about all of the things she wasn't going to talk about in her monologue, like her personal life.

3. **A.** Taylor first appeared on SNL as a musical guest on January 10, 2009. Later that year, on November 7, 2009, she returned to SNL, this time as the host. As of this writing, that was the only time she's hosted the show. However, she's come back a few times over the years to make surprise appearances and cameos in sketches. And she's returned as the musical guest in 2017, 2019, and 2021.

4. **C.** Taylor was in the 2021 SNL digital short "Three Sad Virgins," which starred the comedy trio Please Don't Destroy. In the short, comedian Pete Davidson mocked the PDD guys by singing a song called "Three Sad Virgins." Partway through the song, Taylor unexpectedly appeared and joined Pete in singing the tune.

5. **B.** Simu Liu, star of the 2021 Marvel film *Shang-Chi and the Legend of the Ten Rings.* In February 2024, when talking to a *Variety* reporter about Taylor's many People's Choice Award nominations, Liu revealed that he was in fact a Swiftie. He also complimented Taylor's songwriting skills, and sang a little bit of her song "The Great War."

Reputation Stadium Tour Quiz

Below is a list of cities where Taylor Swift performed during her Reputation Stadium Tour. The only thing is, they've lost all instances of A, E, I, O, U, and Y. Can you figure out the missing vowels and name each city in the list below?

1. P_S_D_N_
2. S__TTL_
3. CH_C_G_
4. M_NCH_ST_R
5. D_BL_N
6. L___SV_LL_
7. C_L_MB_S
8. PH_L_D_LPH__

9. __ST R_TH_RF_RD
10. T_R_NT_
11. _TL_NT_
12. M_NN__P_L_S
13. _RL_NGT_N
14. S_DN__
15. T_K__

More One-Word Titles

Every Taylor Swift song title listed is contained within the group of letters. Titles can be found in a straight line horizontally, vertically, or diagonally. They may be read either forward or backward.

AUGUST	GORGEOUS
BETTY	HAUNTED
BREATHE	INNOCENT
CHANGE	MARJORIE
CLOSURE	MINE
DELICATE	MIRRORBALL
DOROTHEA	STARLIGHT
ENCHANTED	SUPERMAN
EXILE	TREACHEROUS
FEARLESS	UNTOUCHABLE
FLORIDA!!!	WONDERLAND

```
P R S S U O R E H C A E R T N F
W O N D E R L A N D L D N T A U
F L W R I D U D E L I C A U H N
M Y M I N N O C E N T E G A T T
A N B O T M A R J O R U U P H O
R P P E J Y E D O B S N A A G U
J A D C J E R B E T T Y F S I C
O D C H A N U R X L H R S X L H
R I C B R C S E I W I E E D R A
I R L M M H O A L A L C A S A B
E O O T I A L T E R O B A X T L
A L S S E N C H A N G E E T S E
U F U X R T E E N C H A N T E D
G A I O Y X F I H T O R O D T I
U L F Y L L A B R O R R I M W G
S U O E G R O G N A M R E P U S
```

Wildest Dreams

The iconic music video for Swift's hit single "Wildest Dreams" debuted in 2015 as part of Swift's *1989* era. The video, inspired by the film *Out of Africa*, was shot on location in South Africa and Botswana. Following the music video's release, Swift donated all the proceeds to the African Parks Foundation.

Answers on page 150.

FEARLESS

ACROSS

2. First name of Swift's best friend mentioned in "Fifteen"
5. Estate in Tennessee where the *Love Story* music video was shot
7. State in which the first show on the Fearless Tour was played
9. How many songs on the original version of the album did Swift write alone?
12. First single from the album
15. What track was featured on one of Taylor's favorite TV shows, *Grey's Anatomy*?
18. What popular crime drama did Swift guest star in during the *Fearless* era?
20. Taylor's age when the original version of the album was released in 2008
21. The Fearless Tour was Swift's ____ concert tour
22. Collaborator on "Breathe"
23. Taylor wrote "The Best Day" song for her mother, ____
27. Co-producer on "We Were Happy"
28. Featured artist on "That's When"
29. Co-writer of six tracks on the original deluxe version of the album
30. Number of Grammy Awards won by *Fearless*
31. Title of track 4

DOWN

1. Title of track 13
3. Swift emerged at the beginning of the Fearless Tour dressed in a ____ uniform
4. Month when *Fearless (Taylor's Version)* was released
6. Title of track 6
8. *Fearless* helped Swift become the youngest person ever to win this award at the 2010 Grammys
9. How many music videos did Taylor release for the original *Fearless* album (deluxe songs included)?
10. What song has a piano version on the deluxe album?
11. Genre of the album
13. Swift performed "Fifteen" at the 2009 Grammy Awards with what other popular artist?
14. Co-star in the *You Belong with Me* music video
16. Taylor's 2009 *SNL* hosting gig was marked by her "____" from the beginning of the episode
17. Title of track 2
19. Secret message in the album booklet for "Hey Stephen"
24. Even if you have fears and ____, jump
25. Associated album color
26. *Fearless* is which album in her discography?

Emoji Songs

We're searching for a sign. Based on the emojis, guess each Taylor Swift song.

1.

2.

3.

4.

5.

Answers on page 150.

TRIVIA

1. Taylor guest starred in a 2009 episode of *CSI: Crime Scene Investigation*. Her character's name?

   A. Dr. Leigh Sapien

   B. Haley Jones

   C. Meg Wheeler

   D. Sally Roth

2. The title of the 2009 episode of *CSI* in which Taylor appeared was...

   A. "To Have and To Hold"

   B. "The Execution of Catherine Willows"

   C. "Turn, Turn, Turn"

   D. "Primum Non Nocere"

3. What was Taylor's first film appearance (2010)?

   A. Groundhog Day

   B. Mother's Day

   C. New Year's Eve

   D. Valentine's Day

4. What was the name of Taylor's character in the animated film *The Lorax*?

   A. Audrey

   B. Mrs. Wiggins

   C. Aunt Grizelda

   D. Once-ler's Mom

5. In the 2016 animated film *SING*, Rosita (voiced by Reese Witherspoon) wows her family by performing which Taylor Swift song?

   A. "Bad Blood"

   B. "Shake It Off"

   C. "Last Kiss"

   D. "Lavender Haze"

Answers on following page.

1. **B.** Taylor's character Haley Jones is the victim of the episode, and she meets her end in a seedy hotel. Following her demise, the main characters have to solve the murder and figure out what happened to Haley. As more clues come to light, we see flashbacks involving Haley, and Taylor gets to flex her acting muscles!

2. **C.** The episode was called "Turn, Turn, Turn." Taylor's mother Andrea didn't care for the episode, because she didn't like seeing her daughter as the victim in a murder mystery. But Taylor was excited to be a part of the show, because she was a huge fan of CSI!

3. **D.** In the ensemble comedy *Valentine's Day*, Taylor plays a character named Felicia, who's just started dating a guy named Willy (played by Taylor Lautner). Taylor also wrote two songs for the film's soundtrack: "Today Was a Fairytale" and "Jump Then Fall."

4. **A.** In the film, Taylor played Audrey, who was the romantic interest of Ted (played by Zac Efron). The movie *The Lorax* was based on the book of the same name by legendary children's author Dr. Seuss.

5. **B.** Rosita uses Taylor's "Shake It Off" as an empowering anthem to show that there's more to her than others might think. The song's lyrics are all about how you should ignore people's preconceived notions about who you are.

folklore scramble

Unscramble each word or phrase below to reveal a song from Taylor Swift's *folklore* album.

1. THEOCRACY MERITS

2. LET SHAKE

3. BRINIEST LIVINGS

4. TUG U.S.A.

5. IRIS FACIAL LIFT

6. MR. ILL ARBOR

7. HEAT CANADIAN STRATEGY MYRTLES

8. EVENS

9. RACING AD

10. HYGIENIST TRIMS

11. WAND AMMO

12. HYPE PAIN

Answers on page 150.

From the Vault

Every Taylor Swift song title listed is contained within the group of letters. Titles can be found in a straight line horizontally, vertically, or diagonally. They may be read either forward or backward.

BABE

BETTER MAN

BYE BYE BABY

CASTLES CRUMBLING

DON'T YOU

ELECTRIC TOUCH

FOOLISH ONE

FOREVER WINTER

I BET YOU THINK (About Me)

I CAN SEE YOU

IS IT OVER NOW?

MESSAGE IN A BOTTLE

MR. PERFECTLY FINE

NOTHING NEW

NOW THAT WE (Don't Talk)

RUN

SAY DON'T GO

SUBURBAN LEGENDS

THAT'S WHEN

TIMELESS

THE VERY FIRST NIGHT

WE WERE HAPPY

(When Emma) FALLS IN LOVE

YOU ALL OVER ME

```
B B Y E B Y E B A B Y G P Y F T V B
T F S P B F A L L S I N L O V E R D
Y H M U T N O D Y A R I E U T N G O
K I E R B E M R E V O L L A U O Y N
N C S V P U R S E L S B E L O W P T
I A S I E E R N E V G M M L Y T P Y
H N A D L R R B E V E U I O T H A I
T S G P E Y Y F A H R R T V N A H S
U E E N C L F F E N W C W E O T E I
O E I O T S N O I C L S P I D W R T
Y Y N T R A A I O R T E T C N E E O
T O A H I Y M D S L S L G A L T W V
E U B I C D R B A L I T Y E H M E E
B R O N T O E T A R L S N F N T W R
I R T G O N T C U B L A H I I D G N
U R T N U T T N T D K C F O G N S O
U H L E C G E B A B S C M O N H E W
T A E W H O B S S E L E M I T E T B
```

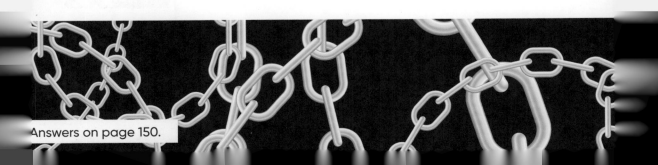

Answers on page 150.

Name the Songs

Guess each Taylor Swift song based on the pictures shown.

1.

2.

3.

Answers on page 150.

Addagram

In addition to being scrambled, each phrase below is missing the same letter. Discover the missing letter, then unscramble the words. When you do, you'll reveal 4 singles from Taylor Swift's *1989* album.

ANCIENT WORM

BANAL PECK

FAKE IF HOT

OUTDO WET HOOF

Matching

Match each Taylor Swift song to the film soundtrack on which the song appeared.

1. "Carolina"
2. "Eyes Open"
3. "I Don't Wanna Live Forever"
4. "Beautiful Ghosts"
5. "Crazier"
6. "Sweeter than Fiction"

A. *Cats*
B. *The Hunger Games*
C. *Where the Crawdads Sing*
D. *One Chance*
E. *Hannah Montana: The Movie*
F. *Fifty Shades Darker*

Answers on pages 150–151.

Speak Now

ACROSS

1. Title of track 11
6. Swift posted a behind the scenes video for the making of the music video for this bonus track
7. *Speak Now* earned this award at the Billboard Awards
12. Associated album color
13. At what age did Taylor re-record this album?
14. July 9 is a day to celebrate this song
15. Month *Speak Now (Taylor's Version)* was released
16. Number of songwriting collaborators on the original album
17. Hit Train song that Swift covered on the Speak Now World Tour, featured on the live album
20. This song regained popularity in 2021/2022 on TikTok, prompting a new wave of "TikTok Swifties"
22. Taylor released this fragrance after the album's release
24. According to Swift, she was between the ages of ___ and twenty when she wrote the original album
26. Actress featured in the *Mean* music video
27. Opening country of the Speak Now World Tour
28. Before the release of "All Too Well (10 Minute Version)," this was Swift's longest song
29. In the beginning of the tour version of "Better than Revenge," a voicemail greeting ends with ___

30. Taylor posted behind the scenes vlogs on her ___ channel during the tour
31. Title of track 8

DOWN

2. This vault track featured Hayley Williams of Paramore
3. How many songs from *Speak Now* were included in the Eras Tour setlist?
4. Dramatic song featuring an orchestra in its studio recording
5. The *I Can See You* music video featured Joey King and ___
8. Which song famously underwent a lyric change upon the release of *Speak Now (Taylor's Version)*?
9. Lead single on the album upon its original release
10. Music video made up of clips from the Speak Now World Tour
11. Closing city of the Speak Now World Tour
13. *Speak Now* is which album in her discography?
18. Number of music videos made for the original album
19. Taylor's version was released this many years after the original
21. Title of track 7
23. Swift used a guitar with this animal on it during the tour
25. Beloved song on *Speak Now* written for Swifties

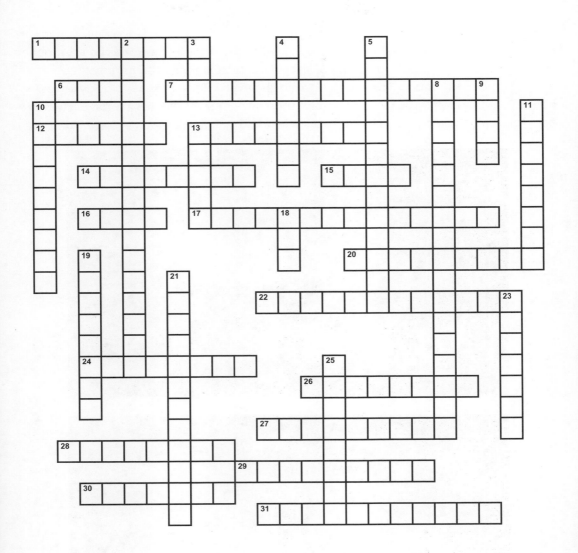

Look What You Made Me Do

Following the release of the lead single from Swift's *reputation* album, the *Look What You Made Me Do* music video helped Swift make a statement on the future of her musical career. Her sound was changing, and she even referred to the "old Taylor" as dead. The video famously features an end scene where Swift dresses in past costumes from tours, music videos, and album eras to send an ever important message.

TRIVIA

1. What is the name of the Nashville performance venue where Taylor was first discovered in 2005?

   A. The Bluebird Café
   B. Tennessee Performing Arts Center
   C. Ryman Auditorium
   D. Cannery Hall

2. Which song was Taylor's 2006 debut single?

   A. "Stay Beautiful"
   B. "Mary's Song"
   C. "Tim McGraw"
   D. "Cold As You"

3. What retail company did Taylor briefly model for in 2003?

   A. Pacsun
   B. Abercrombie & Fitch
   C. Forever 21
   D. Anthropologie

4. How old was Taylor when she got her first deal with a record company?

   A. Eleven
   B. Fourteen
   C. Fifteen
   D. Seventeen

5. On May 6, 2023, during the second night of the Eras Tour in Nashville, Taylor dedicated a performance of this song to a high school friend.

   A. "Never Grow Up"
   B. "Fearless"
   C. "It's Nice to Have a Friend"
   D. "Fifteen"

1. **A.** Back in 2005, Taylor had been invited to sing at the Bluebird Café. The invitation came from her songwriting mentor Liz Rose, who co-wrote some of Taylor's early hits. When Taylor performed at the Bluebird Café that night in 2005, a music industry executive was in the audience, and he was very impressed with Taylor!

2. **C.** Taylor's first single, "Tim McGraw," is about a woman who's recently ended a relationship. And her best memories of that relationship involve the Tim McGraw song she and her ex-boyfriend listened to together. When Taylor was first starting out in the music industry, she looked to husband and wife country music superstars Tim McGraw and Faith Hill as friends and mentors.

3. **B.** Just like celebs Channing Tatum, Emma Roberts, and Jennifer Lawrence, Taylor modeled for Abercrombie & Fitch before she was famous!

4. **B.** Taylor was fourteen years old when she signed an artist development deal at major record label RCA. However, RCA kept her in an artist development deal because they didn't feel ready to commit to an actual record deal. Taylor got tired of waiting for RCA to commit, and eventually, she left the label and signed with SONY/ATV. She was the youngest songwriter they'd ever signed!

5. **D.** In high school, Taylor and Abigail Anderson were best friends, and they've remained close ever since. Taylor was a bridesmaid in Abigail's 2017 wedding. On May 6, 2023, during the second night of the Eras Tour in Nashville, Taylor dedicated a performance of "Fifteen" to Abigail.

Name the Songs

Solve these shrouded mysteries! Guess each Taylor Swift song based on the pictures shown.

1.

2.

3.

Matching

Match each Taylor Swift music video to the person who stars as the love interest in it.

1. *We Are Never Ever Getting Back Together*

2. *Teardrops on My Guitar*

3. *Style*

4. *Wildest Dreams*

5. *Lavender Haze*

6. *Mine*

7. *You Belong with Me*

8. *I Knew You Were Trouble.*

9. *Love Story*

10. *White Horse*

11. *Ours*

A. Lucas Till

B. Zach Gilford

C. Noah Mills

D. Toby Hemingway

E. Reeve Carney

F. Tyler Hilton

G. Stephen Colletti

H. Dominic Sherwood

I. Laith Ashley De La Cruz

J. Justin Gaston

K. Scott Eastwood

Answers on page 151.

Addagram

In addition to being scrambled, each word or phrase below is missing the same letter. Discover the missing letter, then unscramble the words. When you do, you'll reveal 4 Taylor Swift albums.

FOOL ELK   VOLE

TOP AUNTIE   SELF SEA

Matching

Match each bonus track to the Taylor Swift album on which it appeared.

1. "Girl at Home"   A. *Taylor Swift*

2. "I Heart ?"   B. *Fearless*

3. "Wonderland"   C. *Red*

4. "Jump Then Fall"   D. *1989*

Answers on page 151.

evermore scramble

Unscramble each phrase below to reveal a song from Taylor Swift's *evermore* album.

1. OMIT EGOTIST

2. DANCE NOSILY

3. HEAD ROOT

4. MERE ROVE

5. WOW, ILL

6. BEYOND MORONIC

7. TRY SOLO THRONGS

8. MIGHTY FREEWHEEL TOUR

9. SO CRUEL

10. MRS. CHANGEABLE POMP

11. BECOME ILK YOW

12. ROTATE TILE

13. OLD SHRUG

Word Fill-In

Use each of the words and names given to complete this clueless crossword grid. The puzzle has only one solution.

3 letters

CAT
MIC
ONE

4 letters

LOVE
MINE
POET
TUNE

5 letters

CRUEL
MUSIC
STORY
VIDEO
WRITE

6 letters

SUMMER
WILLOW

9 letters

MIDNIGHTS

Find 6 changes

Our Song

The *Our Song* music video premiered in 2006 following the release of Swift's first album, *Taylor Swift*. The video features several scenes in which Swift talks on the phone, paints her nails, sits on the front porch of her house, and lies in a bed of these colorful roses. To this day, the video remains an early favorite among both longtime and newer fans.

Answers on page 152.

Below is a list of surprise covers Taylor Swift played on her Speak Now World Tour. The only thing is, they've lost all instances of A, E, I, O, U, and Y. Can you figure out the missing vowels and name each cover song in the list below?

1. _ _ _ L _ _RN (Alanis Morissette)

2. D_NC_NG _N TH_ D_RK (Bruce Springsteen)

3. L_S_ _ _ _RS_LF (Eminem)

4. _ H_ _RD _T THR_ _GH TH_ GR_P_V_N_ (Marvin Gaye)

5. J_ST _ DR_ _M (Nelly)

6. G_D _NL_ KN_WS (The Beach Boys)

7. S_MM_R _F '69 (Bryan Adams)

8. _NPR_TT_ (TLC)

9. DR_PS _F J_P_T_R (Train)

10. H_W T_ S_V_ _ L_F_ (The Fray)

11. B_B_ G_RL (Sugarland)

12. W_D_ _P_N SP_C_S (The Chicks)

13. _LL _ _ _ W_NT_D (Michelle Branch)

14. CR_ M_ _ R_V_R (Justin Timberlake)

Answers on page 152.

TRIVIA

1. In 2020, Taylor released a Netflix documentary called _____.

   A. Taylor Swift: The Eras Tour

   B. Miss Americana

   C. The Complete Taylor Swift Story

   D. Thank You, America!

2. In the documentary, Taylor confesses she'd never eaten one of these until she was in her late twenties.

   A. Churro

   B. Quesadilla

   C. Taco

   D. Burrito

3. Taylor's friends say that she's quite the chef, especially her tasty _____.

   A. Bolognese sauce

   B. Steak tartare

   C. Crab cakes

   D. Ceviche

4. In 2022, Taylor said that ____ changed her perspective on cooking.

   A. Bobby Flay

   B. Guy Fieri

   C. Ina Garten

   D. Gordon Ramsay

5. Taylor's first professional singing gig was opening for ____.

   A. Asleep at the Wheel

   B. Rascal Flatts

   C. Charlie Daniels Band

   D. Lonestar

Answers on following page.

1. **B.** The documentary was called *Miss Americana*. Through this documentary, Taylor gave fans a glimpse into her private life. Because she allowed director Lana Wilson to film her sessions in the recording studio, the film also gave audiences a peek into Taylor's creative process.

2. **D.** It wasn't until her late twenties that Taylor discovered the joy of burritos. And now that she likes burritos, she likes to put tortilla chips inside them for extra crunchiness. These are but two of the many secrets revealed in the documentary *Miss Americana*.

3. **A.** When Taylor's pal Gigi Hadid was interviewed by *InStyle* in 2023, she revealed that Taylor is really good at making bolognese sauce. She also said that Taylor is an excellent cook in general!

4. **C.** Taylor said that celebrity chef Ina Garten totally changed the way she thought about cooking. Previously, Taylor had thought of cooking as a chore. But after watching Ina cook on her TV series *Barefoot Contessa*, Taylor said that cooking seemed like a relaxing form of self-care.

5. **C.** While still in middle school, Taylor won a karaoke contest at the Pat Garrett Roadhouse. She entered the karaoke contest every weekend for a year and a half until she finally won. The prize was a spot opening for the Charlie Daniels Band. It was Taylor's first professional gig. Shortly afterward, Taylor's family moved closer to Nashville, Tennessee, to pursue her country music dreams.

NYC Scramble

Unscramble each word or phrase below to reveal NYC places mentioned in Taylor Swift songs.

1. GIVE WALLETS
2. MONIED QUASARS
3. BORN YOLK
4. ONLY CANDIES
5. STEADIES
6. WISEST ED

Matching

Match each Taylor Swift song to the band it features.

1. "Soon You'll Get Better"
2. "no body, no crime"
3. "Florida!!!"
4. "coney island"

A. HAIM
B. Florence and the Machine
C. The Chicks
D. The National

Answers on page 152.

Taylor Swift

ACROSS

1. Swift's age when her self-titled album was released
3. Extended play Taylor released in 2008 following her first debut album
4. Title of track 10
6. Last single released off of the album
8. What she never gets to drive in "Picture to Burn"
9. Number of tracks on the original version of the album
11. Swift iconically performed "Should've Said No" at the 2007 ACM Awards in the ___
13. Around the time of this album's release, Swift opened for this popular country musical group on tour
15. Number of musical bonus tracks included in the album's deluxe edition
16. In the *Picture to Burn* music video, Taylor and her best friend, Abigail, sit in what kind of car as they spy on Swift's ex-boyfriend?
18. Genre of the album
20. Swift wrote "Tied Together with a Smile" about a ___
21. The album is formally called *Taylor Swift*, but is known by fans as ___
22. What slams in "Our Song"?
24. Title of track 5
25. Number of songs co-written with Liz Rose on the original version of the album
26. How many non-consecutive weeks did this album top the Billboard Top Country Album chart?

DOWN

2. A few years prior to the album's release, Taylor's family moved from Pennsylvania to the ___ area to pursue her country music ambitions
3. Swift began working on this album around the time she signed with ___
5. Following the release of her debut album, Swift won the ___ at the 2007 CMAs
6. How many music videos did Swift release for the album?
7. She wrote this song for a school talent show and it remains one of her signature hits
10. Swift is expected to release this album as the ___ re-record
12. Track 1 and lead single from album
14. Swift wrote "The Outside" at age ___
17. In the *Teardrops on My Guitar* music video, Swift lounges on a bed in a green ballgown, cradling a ___
19. In the *Our Song* music video, Swift is on the porch of a house wearing an iconic ___ dress
20. Swift wrote most of the songs on this album during her ___ year of high school
21. What is the name of the boy mentioned in "Teardrops on My Guitar"?
23. Release month of *Taylor Swift*

Find the Cats

Can you find doppelgangers of Taylor Swift's 3 cats—Meredith Grey, Olivia Benson, and Benjamin Button—hidden in the picture? Find one? Find yourself another.

Answers on page 153.

Celebrity Scramble

Unscramble each phrase below to reveal a celebrity who appeared in Taylor Swift's *You Need to Calm Down* music video.

1. AU PURL

2. BLAMED A TRAM

3. PERKY TRAY

4. DREARY NYLONS

5. ORCHESTRAL KETCH

6. BROIL PERTLY

7. ENGENDER EL EELS

8. REAL CONVEX

9. JOYFULNESS GREETERS

10. I'M PRO PANDA

11. THICK DOLLAR

12. DEAD LEFTY REMIX

13. TRANCE FAN

Answers on page 153.

Taylor Swift's Influences

Every name listed is contained within the group of letters. Names can be found in a straight line horizontally, vertically, or diagonally. They may be read either forward or backward.

ALANIS MORISSETTE

BEYONCÉ

BRITNEY SPEARS

CARLY SIMON

THE CHICKS

DOLLY PARTON

FAITH HILL

FALL OUT BOY

JAMES TAYLOR

JONI MITCHELL

LEANN RIMES

LINDA RONSTADT

LORETTA LYNN

LORI MCKENNA

MARTINA MCBRIDE

MELISSA ETHERIDGE

PAT BENATAR

PATSY CLINE

PATTY GRIFFIN

PAUL MCCARTNEY

RIHANNA

SARAH MCLACHLAN

SHANIA TWAIN

STEVIE NICKS

TAMMY WYNETTE

TIM MCGRAW

```
F S L E A N N R I M E S W N N O Y E B
L Y O B T U O L L A F M I R N N A E L
S K C I N E I V E T S F E N A H I R H
V F A I T H H I L L F K G V P R B G K
S B U E J Y P F O I O A D N D A K A O
N N Y L A T T E R O L D I A O T F T E
K C P K M E R G I V S C R L L A Y D D
T A R D E T Y N M L R L E H L N E A I
R R I H S T T I C T A L H C Y E N T R
E L R V T E H A K I E E T A P B T S B
N Y A A A N E W E M P H E L A T R N C
I S P N Y Y C T N M S C A C R A A O M
L I Y N L W H A N C Y T S M T P C R A
C M L A O Y I I A G E I S H O S C A N
Y O L H R M C N P R N M I A N G M D I
S N O I D M K A J A T I L R J W L N T
T U D R W A S H K W I N E A T H U I R
A I P E T T E S S I R O M S I N A L A
P E C N O Y E B D G B J T B K S P L M
```

Name the Songs

Guess each Taylor Swift song based on the pictures shown.

1.

2.

3.

  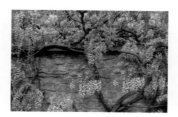 

Answers on page 153.

TRIVIA

1. In 2019, when Taylor appeared on *The Tonight Show*, what clip did host Jimmy Fallon show that surprised her?

   A. A video of her being a guest at a friend's wedding reception

   B. A video of her after eye surgery

   C. A video of her running for student council in high school

   D. A video of her performing in a school play

2. Which cookie is Taylor known for baking?

   A. Pumpkin spice

   B. Chocolate chip

   C. Chai sugar

   D. Red velvet

3. What was the name of Taylor's character in the 2019 movie musical *Cats*?

   A. Victoria

   B. Grizabella

   C. Jennyanydots

   D. Bombalurina

4. Taylor and Ed Sheeran co-wrote which song?

   A. "Everything Has Changed"

   B. "Perfect"

   C. "Blank Space"

   D. "Shape of You"

5. Ed Sheeran was Taylor's opening act during the North American dates of which 2013–2014 tour?

   A. 1989 World Tour

   B. Red Tour

   C. Midnights Tour

   D. Fearless Tour

Answers on following page.

Answers from previous page:

1. **B.** Before the *Tonight Show* episode began, Taylor's mother, Andrea, gave the show's producers a video she'd recorded of Taylor right after she had undergone LASIK eye surgery. Taylor was surprised to see the video broadcast on national TV, but she and Jimmy are friends, so it was okay!

2. **C.** Taylor based her recipe for chai sugar cookies on the one created by popular food blogger Joy Wilson, of the JoyTheBaker blog. She also shared the recipe with fans on Tumblr. As Taylor herself wrote at the end of the recipe, "Cause the bakers gonna bake bake bake bake bake."

3. **D.** Taylor played Bombalurina, who was featured in the number "Macavity: The Mystery Cat," where she told all of the Jellicle cats about the evil Macavity. The 2019 film *Cats* was based on the long-running Broadway musical of the same name.

4. **A.** The song "Everything Has Changed" appeared on Taylor's album *Red* (2012). Taylor and Ed have been friends since 2012.

5. **B.** Ed opened for Taylor during the Red Tour in 2013 and 2014. Before that, in 2012, they'd performed a duet together at Madison Square Garden in New York City, as part of Z100's Jingle Ball.

Starting with "The"

Every Taylor Swift song title starting with "The" listed is contained within the group of letters. Titles can be found in a straight line horizontally, vertically, or diagonally. They may be read either forward or backward.

ALBATROSS

ALCHEMY

ARCHER

BEST DAY

BOLTER

GREAT WAR

LAKES

LAST TIME

LUCKY ONE

MAN

MOMENT I KNEW

OUTSIDE

STORY OF US

WAY I LOVED YOU

```
M  A  W  A  Y  I  L  O  V  E  D  M  U
O  U  T  S  I  D  E  H  C  L  A  O  E
S  S  K  I  T  N  E  M  O  M  Y  M  G
M  S  U  L  A  S  T  T  I  D  K  E  B
I  E  E  F  A  L  C  H  E  M  Y  N  O
R  K  M  H  O  B  B  V  N  A  C  T  L
A  A  I  H  E  Y  O  A  D  A  A  I  T
W  L  T  S  C  L  R  T  T  D  M  K  E
T  B  T  D  I  R  S  O  S  R  E  N  R
A  D  S  Y  V  E  A  B  T  U  O  E  D
E  S  A  L  B  A  T  R  O  S  S  W  K
R  W  L  U  C  K  Y  O  N  E  K  A  L
G  R  U  R  E  H  C  R  A  T  L  O  B
```

RED

ACROSS

1. Deluxe track recalling the story of Swift's boyfriend skipping her 21st birthday party
3. Viral video of this animal screaming is associated with "I Knew You Were Trouble."
5. Where was the *Begin Again* music video filmed?
7. *Red* is often considered Swift's true ____ album
9. Release month of *Red (Taylor's Version)*
10. Title of track 7
13. Featured artist in "Nothing New"
16. Red Tour costume, typically seen at the circus
20. "Maple Latte" is the secret message in the album booklet for which song?
21. Red Tour opening city
22. Taylor made a cameo in this popular sitcom airing during the *Red* era
24. Finish this cryptic line from the *Red* era: Not a lot going on ____
26. What season is *Red* typically associated with?
27. Some people might ask, who's Taylor Swift ___?
28. Which bonus track on *Red (Taylor's Version)* did Swift originally write for the country group Little Big Town?
29. Song inspired by a photo of activist Ethel and senator Bobby Kennedy when they were 17
30. *Red* is which album in her discography?
31. Collaborator on "The Last Time"

DOWN

2. The *22* music video was filmed in this luxurious California city one day after Taylor attended the 55th Grammy Awards
3. Swift earned four ____ nominations for the album
4. Title of track 3
6. She stars in *All Too Well: The Short Film* opposite Dylan O'Brien
8. Band of 31-Across
11. Title of track 10
12. How many bonus tracks were included on *Red (Taylor's Version)*?
14. Director of the *I Bet You Think About Me* music video
15. Which country group did Swift originally write "Babe" for?
17. Taylor's band was dressed as these types of animals in the *We Are Never Ever Getting Back Together* music video
18. An acoustic version of this song is featured on the deluxe album
19. Ed Sheeran surprised Swift onstage during a Red Tour performance dressed as this
23. Which song on the album features "happy sounds" in its chorus?
25. Song associated with cryptic line in 24-Across

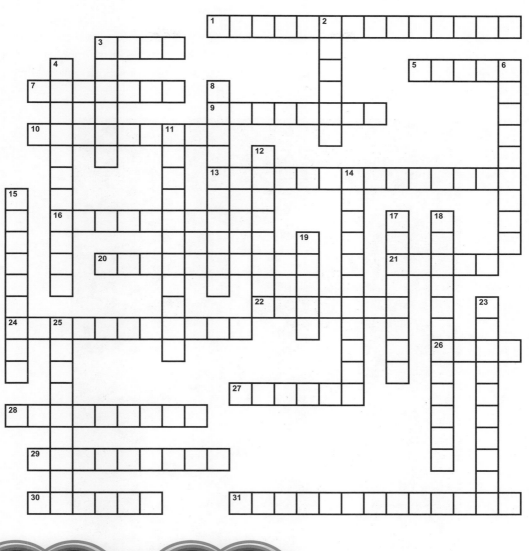

Answers on page 154.

Find 7 changes

Lavender Haze

The sultry *Lavender Haze* music video from Swift's *Midnights* takes viewers through a love story in a futuristic yet nostalgic world. Swift wrote and directed the video and stars opposite actor and model Laith Ashley. *Lavender Haze* features koi fish, an animal first noteworthy to fans from her *Speak Now* album, used again here.

Songwriting Partners

Every songwriting partner of Taylor Swift's listed is contained within the group of letters. Names can be found in a straight line horizontally, vertically, or diagonally. They may be read either forward or backward.

AARON DESSNER	MARK FOSTER
ANGELO PETRAGLIA	MARK SPEARS
BRETT BEAVERS	MARTIN JOHNSON
CAUTIOUS CLAY	MAX MARTIN
COLBIE CAILLAT	NATHAN CHAPMAN
DAN NIGRO	OSCAR HOLTER
DAN WILSON	PAT MONAHAN
DIANE WARREN	RYAN TEDDER
HILLARY LINDSEY	SAM DEW
IMOGEN HEAP	SHELLBACK
JACK ANTONOFF	ST. VINCENT
JACKNIFE LEE	T BONE BURNETT
JAHAAN SWEET	TOMMY LEE JAMES
JOEL LITTLE	WILLIAM BOWERY
LIZ ROSE	ZOË KRAVITZ
LORI MCKENNA	

A C U R M A R K F O S T E R K O R Z I L
P N Z O E K R A V I T Z J W Y U A J Y M
W I R R D N B F F O N O T N A K C A J M
E T Z E Y E S D N I L Y R A L L I H A A
D R V N R P J S L I W N A D C U N A C R
M A T O M M Y L E E J A M E S P Y A K T
A M O R G I N N A D B W Z W U A N N N I
S X T B O N E B U R N E T T O T A S I N
U A M E L T T I L L E O J U I M N W F J
J M S R E V A E B T T E R B T O N E E O
D I A N E W A R R E N D M A U N E E L H
A I L G A R T E P O L E G N A A K T E N
N Z T A L L I A C E I B L O C H C F E S
W T N E C N I V T S Z D M A S A M N J O
I M O G E N H E A P R W D A N N I G A N
L R W I L L I A M B O W E R Y M R I Z W
S E F U K S R A E P S K R A M R O M X Y
O U R Y A N T E D D E R T T I L L E O J
N Z X P U C J N A M P A H C N A H T A N
K C A B L L E H S R E T L O H R A C S O

Name the Songs

Think we can solve them? Guess each Taylor Swift song based on the pictures shown.

1.

2.

3.

Answers on page 154.

TRIVIA

1. Which of Taylor's albums did she release as the first re-recording?

   A. Fearless

   B. 1989

   C. Red

   D. Speak Now

2. Taylor's *All Too Well: The Short Film* opens with a quote from which poet?

   A. Pablo Neruda

   B. Maya Angelou

   C. Robert Frost

   D. Walt Whitman

3. In December 2020, this actor from *The Office* pretended not to know who Taylor was during an online exchange.

   A. John Krasinski

   B. Mindy Kaling

   C. Angela Kinsey

   D. Rainn Wilson

4. The "Swiftposium" academic conference was held for the first time in February 2024 in which major city?

   A. Los Angeles

   B. New York

   C. Melbourne

   D. Tokyo

5. For which album did Taylor win the 2024 Album of the Year Grammy?

   A. evermore

   B. 1989

   C. Midnights

   D. folklore

Answers on following page.

1. **A.** The 2021 release *Fearless (Taylor's Version)* was the first "Taylor's Version" she released. A few years ago, Taylor undertook a massive project. She re-recorded her early albums so that she could own the masters. The "Taylor's Version" albums were the result.

2. **A.** *All Too Well: The Short Film*, which Taylor directed, opens with the following quote from Chilean poet Pablo Neruda: "Love is so short, forgetting is so long."

3. **D.** In 2020, Taylor, a longtime fan of *The Office*, used a gif of Rainn Wilson as his *Office* character Dwight Schrute to respond to a headline about her album *evermore*. And in response to that, Wilson tweeted the following about the famous pop star: "I do not know who this is. Inventor of the Swiffer?" Taylor replied with a gif of another *Office* character saying, "Touché."

4. **C.** The Swiftposium academic summit in Melbourne, which preceded the Eras Tour in Australia, attracted participants from all over the world. They were there to examine Taylor's career, her music, and her impact on pop culture. The event was organized by scholars from six universities across Australia and New Zealand.

5. **C.** At the 2024 Grammy Awards, Taylor won the Album of the Year Award for her 2022 album *Midnights*. This gave her four Album of the Year wins, the most for any single artist in Grammy history.

RED Tour Quiz

Are you a mastermind? Below is a list of opening acts for Taylor Swift's Red Tour. The only thing is, they've lost all instances of A, E, I, O, U, and Y. Can you figure out the missing vowels and name each opening act in the list below?

1. _D SH__R_N

2. BR_TT _LDR_DG_

3. __ST_N M_H_N_

4. FL_R_D_ G__RG__ L_N_

5. J__L CR__S_

6. C_S__ J_M_S

7. N__N TR__S

8. G__ S_B_ST__N

9. TH_ V_MPS

10. _NDR__S B__R_N_

folklore

ACROSS

7. Title of track 10
8. Title of the album's singular bonus track
9. Names of Blake Lively's children, in order of their appearance in track 14
11. Swift performed a mashup of "august," "willow," and ____ at the 2020 Grammys
13. Taylor emotionally compares herself to this object in track 6
15. Song that has underlying parallels to *reputation*'s "I Did Something Bad"
16. How many songs on the album were co-written with William Bowery?
20. Associated album color
21. Which song touches on the life experiences of Swift's late grandfather?
23. "cardigan," "betty," and ____ are the 3 songs that tell the story of a love triangle
27. What song on *Red* did Taylor compare the feel of *folklore* to?
28. Collaborator and featured artist on "exile"
29. Title of track 15
30. The original name of the "cardigan" sketch Aaron Dessner sent to Swift
31. Location of Swift's house described in "the last great american dynasty," often the location of her 4th of July parties
32. "seven" recalls the struggles of a friend from Taylor's ____

DOWN

1. Name of Swift's makeshift at-home recording studio where part of the album was recorded
2. The first song written for the album, also the only one Taylor wrote alone
3. Number of songs on the original version of the album
4. Swift wrote the stories included in *folklore*, and told fans it's now up to them to ____.
5. "the last great american dynasty" retold the life of Rebekah ____
6. *folklore*'s sister album
10. Month *folklore* was released
12. Swift won her third ____ award at the 2021 Grammys for *folklore*
14. Director of the *cardigan* music video
17. *folklore* is which album in her discography?
18. The album was entirely written and recorded during ____
19. Swift announced the surprise release of *folklore* just ____ day(s) before its release
22. How many editions of the album did Taylor end up releasing?
24. Swift was purposeful with Easter Eggs in *folklore*, commenting that she left them in the ____
25. Season associated with the album
26. "the 1" and ____ were the last songs to be written for the album
27. *folklore* is Swift's ____ album to include expletives

Shake It Off

Perhaps one of Swift's most involved music videos to date, *Shake It Off* has garnered over 3.4 billion views on YouTube since its release in 2014. This song from *1989* has come to be known as one of Swift's all-time hits, and the video certainly seems to do it justice. Featuring professional dancers and cheerleaders of all styles, this video isn't one to miss!

Answers on page 155.

Lover Scramble

Unscramble each word or phrase below to reveal a song from Taylor Swift's *Lover* album.

1. ANTHEM

2. DEAF LOGS

3. BE GENTLER, LOUSY TOOT

4. AS UNATTACHED BOYS THUD

5. GREAT WOLF

6. RUE MR. MUSCLE

7. HEAR RETCH

8. A WOODENLY DOCUMENT

9. RECREATE TONSIL

10. REAP SPRING

11. A CAD INVENTORIES THIEF

12. LOONY BOND

13. HIKE THINS WONK

14. BREACH THIRTEEN ARMIES & A MANIAC'S PERK

Answers on page 155.

Oh That Vocabulary!

Every word listed is contained within the group of letters. Words can be found in a straight line horizontally, vertically, or diagonally. They may be read either forward or backward.

ALTRUISM	GAUCHE
ANTITHETICAL	ILLICIT
AURORAS	INCANDESCENT
CALAMITOUS	INGENUE
CAPTIVATED	MACHIAVELLIAN
CASCADE	MERCURIAL
CIVILITY	NARCISSISM
CLANDESTINE	NONCHALANT
CONDESCENDING	OPACITY
CONTRARIAN	PEDIGREE
CRESTFALLEN	PERIPHERY
CYNIC	PRECIPICE
DISPOSITION	REVELERS
DWINDLE	SABOTAGE
ELEGIES	TREACHEROUS
EPIPHANY	UNMOORED

H H N O N C H A L A N T C A L T R U I R
D I N C A N D E S C E N T A V I T P A C
E G Y I T E H T I F N A G A U C H E P A R
R D T C L A N D E S T I N G E N U E E S
O G I I C O N D E S C E N D I N G W R C
O I L L I C A P O P E D I G R E E L I A
M C I N Y C L A N D E S T I N E T S P M
N W V I S T S R E L E V E R A C R D H A
U N I A N E L L A F T S E R C V E I E C
L A C I T E H T I T N A U R O R A S R H
T E A A R G L I F I D L I D N F C P Y I
L C L E P A P E C W N T G W T Y H O F A
A I A P N T R C G I G R E I R T E S I V
I P M I E O I T U I V U L N A I R I L E
R I I P G B D V N A E I E D R C O T L L
U C T H N A S D A O G S L A I A U I I L
C E O A I S G Y A T C M U I A P S O C I
R R U Y N A H P I P E R W B N O B N I A
E P S R E I N Y C P O D W I N D L E T N
M S M S I S S I C R A N O T I M A L A C

Matching

Match each Taylor Swift song to the place name mentioned in it.

1. "dorothea"

2. "Tim McGraw"

3. "seven"

4. "I Bet You Think About Me"

5. "The Man"

A. Saint-Tropez

B. Beverly Hills

C. Tupelo

D. Pennsylvania

E. Georgia

Addagram

In addition to being scrambled, each phrase below is missing the same letter. Discover the missing letter, then unscramble the words. When you do, you'll reveal 4 singles from Taylor Swift's *reputation* album.

MEN AGE

EASY YAWNER

TILE ACE

FAIRER TOY

Answers on page 155.

TRIVIA

1. Taylor is the first songwriter in Grammy history to get ____ Song of the Year nominations.

   A. Eight

   B. Six

   C. Five

   D. Seven

2. During her 1989 World Tour, who did NOT join Taylor onstage to perform?

   A. Avril Lavigne

   B. Britney Spears

   C. Steven Tyler

   D. Nick Jonas

3. Taylor is the first living recording artist to have ____ Top 10 albums on the Billboard 200 chart *at the same time*.

   A. Three

   B. Four

   C. Five

   D. Six

4. At the 2024 Grammy Awards, what famous songstress presented an award to Taylor?

   A. Celine Dion

   B. Beyoncé Knowles

   C. Janet Jackson

   D. Cher

5. In November 2023, Taylor tied with ____ for the most Billboard Music Awards of all time.

   A. SZA

   B. Drake

   C. Lady Gaga

   D. Morgan Wallen

Answers on following page.

1. **D.** Taylor has notched a whopping seven Song of the Year Grammy nominations as of this writing. That's one more nomination than six-time nominees—and fellow music-industry titans—Lionel Richie and Paul McCartney.

2. **B.** During her 1989 World Tour in 2015, Taylor brought a slew of superstar special guests onstage to perform with her, including Avril Lavigne, Steven Tyler, Nick Jonas, Mick Jagger, Justin Timberlake, Lorde, The Weeknd, Alanis Morissette, and John Legend. Taylor performed Avril Lavigne's 2002 hit "Complicated" with the Canadian singer in San Diego; Aerosmith's 1998 hit ballad "I Don't Want to Miss a Thing" with frontman Steven Tyler in Nashville; and Nick Jonas's song "Jealous" with him in East Rutherford, New Jersey.

3. **C.** Taylor is the first living artist in the past sixty years to have five Top 10 albums charting simultaneously on the Billboard 200. The only artist to do so before her was Prince, who accomplished the feat in the week following his death.

4. **A.** When Taylor won the 2024 Album of the Year Award for her 2022 album *Midnights*, Celine Dion was the person who presented Taylor with that award. Afterward, Taylor hugged Celine backstage.

5. **B.** Taylor is tied with Drake. As of this writing, each of them has won 39 Billboard Music Awards. In 2023 alone, Taylor took home 10 BBMAs.

Begin Again

Find 8 changes

The pastel, dreamy video from Swift's *Red* album was shot on location in Paris, France. The video was posted to YouTube a day after the album was released on October 22, 2012. In the video, we see Swift taking in iconic Paris views and sitting innocently in a neighborhood café.

Recording Studios

Every recording studio listed is contained within the group of letters. Words can be found in a straight line horizontally, vertically, or diagonally. They may be read either forward or backward.

AUDU

BALLROOM WEST

BIG MERCY

BLACKBIRD

CONWAY

(The) **DWELLING**

EBC

ELECTRIC LADY

GARAGE

GOLDEN AGE

HENSON RECORDING

(The) **HIDEAWAY**

HUTCHINSON SOUND

INSTRUMENT LANDING

KITTY COMMITTEE

LONG POND

METROPOLIS

MXM

PAIN IN THE ART

PLEASURE HILL

PRIME RECORDING

QUAD

ROUGH CUSTOMER

RUBY RED

SHARP SONICS

SOUND EMPORIUM

STARSTRUCK

TREE SOUND

VILLAGE

```
Q D N M E T R O P O L I S A M T Y O N E P
I K C U R T S R A T S Y A W N O C M W N K
Y P U N G N I D N A L T N E M U R T S N I
M U X G N I D R O C E R N O S N E H I V T
P U P R I M E R E C O R D I N G M T L W T
B A I R G Y R Y B U R E G A R A G V L W Y
A I I R D C D X T I Y A W A E D I H E N C
S E G N O N B A D R I B K C A L B L W O O
P H R M I P U A L T M H A M M C A V D C M
S L A E E N M O R C X C U X N V L U B B M
H W E R M R T E S A I H D V A O L G D D I
A A M A P O E H D N G R S B N M R G W U T
R Y N O S S T H E N O R T G E V O G E L T
P Q K E O U O S D A U S P C X I O Q L C E
S U Q U D R R N U T R O N S E L M E L I E
O D N D M L L E D C N T S I D L W Q I R Q
N D U P Y T O L H D H G Q E H A E H N T U
I O P G N O L G A I G G N A E C S B G C A
C D E R Y B U R W B L A U D Q M T M C E D
S L B V I L L A G E G L I O L X Q U D L G
I B K C A L B R S E R H Y K R M W E H E K
```

Speak Now Scramble

Unscramble each word or phrase below to reveal a song from the *Speak Now (Taylor's Version)* album.

1. FOSTERS YOUTH

2. NAME

3. JADE HORN

4. IN ME

5. HAD TUNE

6. THEN DANCE

7. PRY FLASKS

8. TENTH BEVERAGE RENT

9. MEET CABBED CORK

10. OVERGREW PUN

11. ASK LISTS

12. OVEN GILL

13. APE KNOWS

14. MARE SPUN

15. CAB CRUSTING SMELL

Answers on page 156.

Word Fill-In

Use each of the words given to complete this clueless crossword grid. The puzzle has only one solution.

3 letters

BAD
OFF
POP

4 letters

FOLK
SING

5 letters

ALBUM
BLOOD
INDIE
LOVER
SHAKE
TITLE
TRACK
VOICE

6 letters

GRAMMY

7 letters

RELEASE

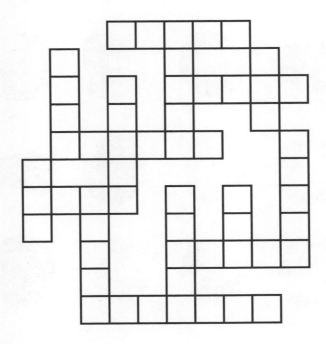

Answers on page 156.

Find 8 changes

Bejeweled

Swift's *Bejeweled* music video meets the criteria for all things glitz, glamor, and old Hollywood. The video features the HAIM sisters and Laura Dern. Burlesque dancer Dita Von Teese is also featured in a classy cabaret set in which she and Swift lay in oversized martini glasses. In true Taylor Swift fashion, *Bejeweled* is full of Easter Eggs for Swift's upcoming projects.

Name the Songs

Guess each Taylor Swift song based on the pictures shown.

1.

2.

3.

Answers on page 156.

TRIVIA

1. In May 2022, Taylor delivered an inspiring commencement address at...

   A. New England Conservatory of Music   C. Juilliard School

   B. Harvard University   D. New York University

2. Taylor's song "Tim McGraw" peaked at number _____ on the country charts.

   A. Six   C. Nine

   B. Five   D. Seven

3. In the 2022 animated film *The DC League of Super-Pets*, when Krypto the super-dog gets upset, which Taylor Swift song does the put-upon pooch blast to blow off steam?

   A. "I Forgot That You Existed"   C. "Bad Blood"

   B. "We Are Never Ever Getting Back Together"   D. "Mad Woman"

4. In the music video for Taylor's song "Look What You Made Me Do," she appears as what kind of classic movie monster?

   A. Vampire   C. Werewolf

   B. Zombie   D. Ghost

5. Who played the titular man in the music video for Taylor's song "The Man"?

Answers on following page.

1. **D.** Taylor gave the address at NYU, where she was awarded an honorary doctorate of fine arts. During her address, Taylor offered uplifting words to the graduates and reflected on the ups and downs of her career so far.

2. **A.** The song peaked at number six on the country music charts. "Tim McGraw" was one of Taylor's earliest musical compositions, since she wrote the song in math class during her freshman year of high school!

3. **C.** In that scene, Krypto listens to "Bad Blood." However, it's not the original version from her 2014 album 1989. Instead, it's the "Taylor's Version" re-recording of the song. However, since Taylor hadn't yet recorded 1989 (Taylor's Version) when League of Super-Pets was in production, she recorded her version of "Bad Blood" for the filmmakers to use in the film, making it the first song to be re-recorded for 1989 (Taylor's Version)!

4. **B.** In a graveyard at the beginning of the video, a zombified Taylor crawls out of a grave and begins singing "Look What You Made Me Do." The headstone atop the grave bears the following inscription: "Here Lies Taylor Swift's Reputation."

5. Thanks to makeup and prosthetics, Taylor portrayed the cigar-smoking male business executive herself! The official music video for "The Man," released on February 27, 2020, was Taylor's solo directorial debut.

RED Scramble

Unscramble each phrase below to reveal a song from the *Red (Taylor's Version)* album.

1. OUR TEACHERS

2. BIWEEKLY UNTRUE WOOER

3. GLORY HOUND

4. EMIT STEALTH

5. SAFER COTTAGE

6. REGRET HOT EAVE; BEGAN VIGNETTE WRECKER

7. A FABRICATED LUG SUIT

8. TOUCH KEENLY

9. ANGINA GIBE

10. TOO DISMAL

11. CHARGE A SEVENTH DINGHY

12. HALTS TRIG

13. EVERYTHING THRIFTS

14. EEK... BEACHCOMBER

15. AMBER TENT

Answers on page 157.

Lover

ACROSS

3. Designer who Swift collaborated with during the *Lover* era
8. How many songs on the album mention the color blue?
10. Title of track 6
13. Title of track 16
14. Taylor's father, Scott, was featured in which music video from the album?
15. This album can be thought of as a ___ to love
16. Street in NYC Swift once lived on, now a popular tourist destination
17. *Lover* is which album in her discography?
19. What do you need ME to spell?
20. Collaborator and featured artist on "ME!"
21. How many versions of the deluxe album did Swift release?
22. Producer and co-writer of "Death by a Thousand Cuts"
24. Name of *Lover* album tour that was canceled due to the Covid-19 pandemic
25. How many different locations in and around London does Swift reference in "London Boy"?
26. *Lover: Live From* ___ is Swift's third live album released
29. How many songs on the album did Taylor write alone?
31. Celebrity whose voice is featured at the beginning of "London Boy"
32. Celebrity dressed as a hamburger in the *You Need to Calm Down* music video

33. Featured group on "Soon You'll Get Better"

DOWN

1. Taylor's iconic line at the beginning of the *ME!* music video
2. The original name for the album was going to be ___
4. Name of Taylor's Netflix documentary that came out in 2020
5. Secret Sessions for the album were held in London, Los Angeles, and ___
6. Name of cat Taylor adopted after meeting on the set of the *ME!* music video
7. "All of the Girls ___" is a vault/bonus track that Swift later released in 2023
9. Number of tracks on the original album
11. Track released as the album's first promotional single
12. Before *Lover*, how many of her albums did Taylor own the masters to?
17. "Death by a Thousand Cuts" was inspired by what Netflix film?
18. Song on *1989* that inspired the concept for the *Lover* music video
23. Swift performed "Lover" and ___ on *SNL* in 2019
27. *Lover* release month
28. Associated album color
30. Depictions of love in "Daylight" are often compared to those in which of Swift's earlier albums?

Answers on page 157.

Addagram

Can you make sense of something crazy? In addition to being scrambled, each phrase below is missing the same letter. Discover the missing letter, then unscramble the words. When you do, you'll reveal 10 Taylor Swift songs.

BARN HILT

MATCH HEEL

LIONS DANCE

SOFTER SHOUT

I HAPPEN

WE LIKE COMBO

TRIMS NIGHTIES

HAD GILT

COMBINE DONOR

ALIGNS SUIT

Answers on page 157.

Find the Cats

We're playing hide-and-seek. Can you find doppelgangers of Taylor Swift's 3 cats—
Meredith Grey, Olivia Benson, and Benjamin Button—hidden in the picture?

Answers on page 157.

Underrated Songs

Every Taylor Swift song title listed is contained within the group of letters. Titles can be found in a straight line horizontally, vertically, or diagonally. They may be read either forward or backward.

BEAUTIFUL EYES

BREATHE

CHANGE

CLOSURE

CRAZIER

DEAR READER

EPIPHANY

HAPPINESS

HEY STEPHEN

HOAX

I ALMOST DO

I KNOW PLACES

INNOCENT

INVISIBLE

IT'S TIME TO GO

JUMP THEN FALL

LAST KISS

THE LAST TIME

THE LUCKY ONE

THE OUTSIDE

SAD BEAUTIFUL TRAGIC

SO IT GOES

STARLIGHT

STATE OF GRACE

STAY BEAUTIFUL

STAY STAY STAY

SUPERMAN

SUPERSTAR

THIS LOVE

TREACHEROUS

UNTOUCHABLE

A E S E I C O T T H E L U C K Y O N E R
I H U D K L S H W H C S O I T G O E S M
N T P I N O S G S I A R H G E D H J A S
V A E S O S E I E T R E A C H E R O U S
I E R T W U N L C A G I P S G A D P Z H
S R M U P R I R A Y F Z P S B R E A T I
I B A O L E P A L S O A I I I R X J S N
B T N E A L P T P T E R N K S E A L U V
L H S H V L A S W A T C E T E A O U P I
O E R T T U H F O Y A N A S Y D H F E S
D L L O I I E E N S T Y H A E E D I R I
T A Y B C M G P K E S H I L L R E T S B
S S E W A N E K I T H N Z E U C V U T L
O T E R A H H T A P N T C D F R O A A E
M T J H R I C Y O O H O P C I A L E R S
L I C F S A S U C G N A H M T Z S B C O
A M R L A T E E O N O A N B U I I Y L I
I E O O A J N D I T N P E Y A J H A O T
K H E Y S T E P H E N Y X R E A T T S G
C I G A R T L U F I T U A E B D A S U O

Name the Songs

Guess each Taylor Swift song based on the pictures shown.

1.

2.

3.

Answers on page 158.

TRIVIA

1. The songs and images of Taylor's album *folklore* are usually considered an example of what style?

   A. Rock opera   C. Punk rock

   B. Cottagecore   D. Fairycore

2. Which popular stand-up comedian plays Taylor's adult son Preston who reads her will in the *Anti-Hero* music video?

   A. Pete Holmes   C. Mike Birbiglia

   B. Jerry Seinfeld   D. Jim Gaffigan

3. In December 2017, Taylor was featured on the cover of _____ *Magazine*'s "Person of the Year" issue, where she was named a "silence breaker."

   A. TIME   C. People

   B. Newsweek   D. Rolling Stone

4. In the music video for "Bad Blood," Taylor played a _____.

   A. Spy   C. Archaeologist

   B. Superhero   D. Detective

5. Taylor's middle name is...

   A. Andrea   C. Elise

   B. Olivia   D. Alison

Answers on following page.

1. **B.** The songs and images for folklore are often categorized as an example of "cottagecore," a style of art and music which involves idealized images of forests, farm houses, autumn leaves, and other iconography calling to mind a fanciful, picture-perfect rural lifestyle.

2. **C.** Mike Birbiglia plays Preston in a scene set several decades in the future when Taylor's greedy, selfish adult children have assembled for her funeral. Birbiglia, as Preston, is the one who reads the will. Taylor's other future children are played by Birbiglia's fellow comedians Mary Elizabeth Ellis and John Early. In the scene described above, Ellis is wearing one of Swift's dresses worn during the Fearless tour!

3. **A.** In 2017, TIME Magazine decided to name a collective of people—silence breakers—as its Person(s) of the Year, rather than a single person. As that issue of TIME explained, silence breakers are people who bravely stepped forth to expose horrible things done by powerful men. Earlier that year, Taylor had spoken out, and won a court battle against, a DJ who'd inappropriately touched her at a public event.

4. **A.** Taylor plays a spy code-named "Catastrophe" in the music video. The video features action movie tropes like the double-crossing best friend, agents with silly code-names, and James Bond-style high tech gadgets.

5. **D.** Taylor's full name is Taylor Alison Swift. Taylor was born on December 13, 1989, in West Reading, Pennsylvania.

Emoji Songs

Based on the emojis, guess each Taylor Swift song.

1.

2.

3.

4.

5.

6.

1989 SCRAMBLE

Unscramble each word or phrase below to reveal a song from the *1989 (Taylor's Version)* album.

1. A BOLD BOD

2. REWEIGH UGLY TOOTH

3. SHOVEL IT

4. OWNS A PICKLE

5. REMITS SWADDLE

6. LANCE

7. KNOW WOOL CEMETERY

8. OUT AS ODD LAYAWAY SLOTH

9. BLACK ASPEN

10. HIS TAKEOFF

11. WOOS FOOTED HUT

12. MISCREANT WON

13. A HOT TWIT'S INFERENCE

14. WHATNOT LAW KNOTTED

15. SUNBURNED BAGELS

Answers on page 158.

Word Fill-In

Use each of the words, names, and acronyms given to complete this clueless crossword grid. The puzzle has only one solution.

3 letters

ART
DVD
FAN

4 letters

ERAS
FILM

HOME
OURS
STAR

5 letters

BONUS
COVER
SWIFT

6 letters

DREAMS
RECORD
TAYLOR

7 letters

CONCERT

ERAS TOUR

ACROSS

3. In what city did fans cause an earthquake while dancing to "Shake It Off"?
4. When brought out as an Eras Tour surprise guest, Taylor Lautner made his entrance doing this
7. What era does Swift begin the show with?
8. Release month of *Taylor Swift: The Eras Tour* film
9. Eras is Swift's ___ world tour
12. Number of songs on the setlist
15. Month the Eras Tour kicked off
16. Song in which fans chant "Take Me to Church!"
17. Swift has three main stages in the show: the Main Stage, the Diamond Stage, and the ___
21. What is Swift's *evermore* era piano covered in?
22. During what song does Swift hand out a signed hat to a fan?
25. Ticket seller website that famously crashed when millions of fans logged on to buy tickets to the Eras Tour
26. During what song with lyrics about a plane did an actual plane fly behind Taylor during the show?
27. In what city did Aaron Dessner join Swift onstage to sing "ivy"?
30. The guy on the ___ is Karma too
31. City in which Swift announced *Speak Now (Taylor's Version)*
32. In what city did Swift announce *1989 (Taylor's Version)*?
33. City in Australia with the biggest fan turnout at the Eras Tour

DOWN

1. First name of the second dancer featured during "Bejeweled"
2. How many shows did Swift play during the 2023 U.S. leg of the tour?
5. Song in which Taylor famously swings a golf club
6. Even though you don't have to, can ___?
10. Opening city on the Eras Tour
11. Swifties make, trade, and wear these to the Eras Tour shows
13. Swift's ___ bedazzled her guitars used in the show
14. How many wardrobe changes are in the show?
15. Choreographer for the tour
16. Swift's ___ album was the only one not featured in the setlist
18. By the end of its run, how many countries will the Eras Tour have visited?
19. Country in which Swift began performing mashup surprise songs
20. Song in which fans chanted "1, 2, 3, LGB!"
23. What era does Swift end the show with?
24. To train for the intensity of tour, Taylor sang every song on the setlist while on a ___
28. Arlington Night 1 surprise song, in addition to "Death by a Thousand Cuts"
29. Number of albums the Eras Tour celebrates

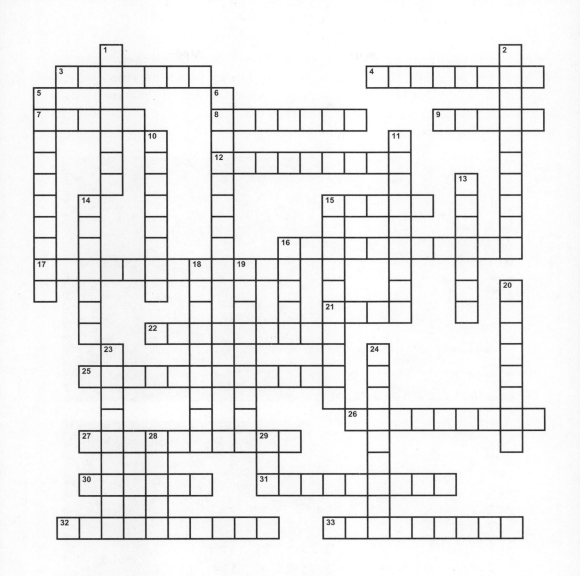

I Can See You

The *I Can See You* music video shocked fans with its sudden premiere during an Eras Tour show in Kansas City, Missouri, in July 2023. Swift's co-stars in the video include Joey King and Taylor Lautner, both of whom she worked with when this vault song was written. The song quickly became a fan favorite after its release on *Speak Now (Taylor's Version)*, and its video surely does not disappoint.

TRIVIA

1. When Taylor was ___ years old, she sang "The Star-Spangled Banner" before a Philadelphia 76ers NBA Finals basketball game.

   A. Twelve

   B. Seven

   C. Eight

   D. Fourteen

2. Early in her career, Taylor opened for _____ on their 2006 arena tour.

   A. The Chicks

   B. The Wreckers

   C. Rascal Flatts

   D. Imagine Dragons

3. In November 2007, Taylor received the _____ Award for best new artist from the Country Music Association.

   A. Horizon

   B. Female Vocalist of the Year

   C. Entertainer of the Year

   D. Newcomer

4. In 2023, Taylor appeared on _____ Magazine's list of most powerful women.

   A. Business Insider

   B. Forbes

   C. The Wall Street Journal

   D. Money

5. In 2024, Taylor made newspaper headlines after it was revealed that she made homemade _____ for the Kansas City Chiefs offensive linemen.

   A. Popcorn

   B. Fritos

   C. Donuts

   D. Pop Tarts

Answers on following page.

1. **A.** Taylor was just twelve years old at the time. She sang the famous song before a crowd of 20,000 people in April 2002.

2. **C.** When Rascal Flatts had a disagreement with their opening act, country star Eric Church, they needed a new opener. Taylor Swift to the rescue! She was their new opening act. And as a show of goodwill towards Eric Church, she gave him her first gold record!

3. **A.** She won the CMA's prestigious Horizon Award. This was a great way to end an incredible year in which Taylor opened for such country music legends as Tim McGraw, Faith Hill, George Strait, and Kenny Chesney.

4. **B.** Taylor was number five on Forbes' list of the most powerful women of 2023. And that same year, a Bloomberg analysis recognized Taylor as a billionaire, with a net worth of $1.1 billion.

5. **D.** She made homemade Pop Tarts for the hardworking athletes. And after word got out that she did this, the Kellogg's brand, the company behind Pop Tarts, took out a full-page ad in the Kansas City Star, asking Taylor to share her recipe!

Midnights Scramble

Unscramble each word or phrase below to reveal a song from Taylor Swift's *Midnights* album.

1. BAR THINLY
2. PAIRS
3. REDDER AREA
4. ONE QUITS
5. DEFINES THRIFT
6. WHETHER A GHOSTLY KING BE
7. ANOTHER I
8. HAZARD ELEVEN
9. REMAND MIST
10. ADMIRING HINT
11. CLOUD EVOLVED DUE LUSH VOW
12. DONKEY RUIN YOUR WOO
13. A MARK
14. ROAM ON
15. HONE OWN BATCHES
16. OWNS TEETHING

Answers on page 158.

Colorful Songs

Each of these Taylor Swift songs that mentions color is contained within the group of letters. Songs can be found in a straight line horizontally, vertically, or diagonally. They may be read either forward or backward.

AFTERGLOW

ALL TOO WELL

THE BEST DAY

BYE BYE BABY

COLD AS YOU

CRUEL SUMMER

DAYLIGHT

DELICATE

END GAME

GETAWAY CAR

GOLD RUSH

GORGEOUS

THE GREAT WAR

HAPPINESS

HOAX

HOLY GROUND

I KNOW PLACES

INVISIBLE STRING

IS IT OVER NOW?

THE LAKES

LOVER

NOTHING NEW

PAPER RINGS

QUESTION

RED

RUN

SNOW ON THE BEACH

SO IT GOES

SPARKS FLY

STYLE

THIS LOVE

TIM MCGRAW

WONDERLAND

```
T I M M C G R A W I S I T O V E R N O W
R G N I R T S E L B I S I V N I C Y E A
X E D O R A W T A E R G E H T Y H M H B
S L D S G S E C A L P W O N K I A T O E
N O O L L E W O O T L L A X I G N H A Y
O V P Y L F S K R A P S F E D P D E V B
W E N G N I H T O N C A T N P S P L Q E
O R E W O O T L L A B Y E B Y E B A B Y
N T H E B E S T D A Y U R D L O G K H B
T H P R A C Y A W A T E G O L D R U S H
H Q T H E L A K E S X O L H X L Y T S Q
E R E M M U S L E U R C O L D A S Y O U
B P A P E R R I N G S L W E A G A G T E
E A C C U I A S E C Y H L C Y O D G H S
A R D R Y F T O P G S I I D L R L D I T
C U N K T Y U S R F C L N A I G O N S I
H T U E L S E O M A E N F Y G E C E L O
A Y R E Y V U U T D O B B L H O A X O N
K G B W O N D E R L A N D I T E R D V P
L A R L D L N A R Q S E O G T I O S E H
```

Answers on page 159.

1989 WORLD TOUR QUIZ

Below is the setlist from Taylor Swift's 1989 World Tour. The only thing is, they've lost all instances of A, E, I, O, U, and Y. Can you figure out the missing vowels and name each song in the setlist below?

1. W_LC_M_ T_ N_W __RK
2. N_W R_M_NT_CS
3. BL_NK SP_C_
4. _ KN_W ___ W_R_ TR__BL_.
5. _ W_SH ___ W__LD
6. H_W ___ G_T TH_ G_RL
7. _ KN_W PL_C_S
8. _LL ___ H_D T_ D_ W_S ST__
9. ___ _R_ _N L_V_
10. CL__N
11. L_V_ ST_R_
12. ST_L_
13. TH_S L_V_
14. B_D BL__D
15. W_ _R_ N_V_R _V_R G_TT_NG B_CK T_G_TH_R
16. _NCH_NT_D/W_LD_ST DR__MS
17. __T _F TH_ W__DS
18. SH_K_ _T _FF

Answers on page 159.

Name the Songs

Guess each Taylor Swift song based on the pictures shown.

1.

2.

3.

Answers on page 159.

Fan Theories

ACROSS

2. Fans believed *1989 (Taylor's Version)* was going to be a double album because of clues left in what music video?
13. Title of supposed third sister album of *folklore* and *evermore*
14. Fans are convinced *Argylle* author ____ is actually Swift writing under a pseudonym
15. Swifties are convinced that "But Daddy I Love Him" is a reference to what Disney film?
18. What song on *evermore* sparked engagement rumors among fans?
19. Fans know that Taylor begins hiding Easter Eggs ____ years in advance
22. During Swift's public hiatus just before *reputation* was released, fans were convinced that she traveled around in a ____ to avoid being seen
24. Title of the rumored "lost" album
25. Fans were convinced that the five versions of *The Tortured Poets Department* represented the ____
26. Fans believe that *evermore* is partly inspired by/dedicated to what famous female poet?

DOWN

1. Animal in a *The Tortured Poets Department* song title that fans theorize is a metaphor for one of her past relationships
3. Fans thought Swift was involved with this movie during the *reputation* era due to the fact that she released a song by the same name

4. When Swift released this *1989* song in a TV trailer, fans were convinced *1989 (Taylor's Version)* was going to be announced
5. Name from a famous Tumblr meme
6. *evermore* is Swift's ____ album
7. The glitch in Taylor's 2021 TikTok to this song caused panic and frenzy among Swifties worldwide
8. Fans were convinced that *reputation (Taylor's Version)* would be released on what holiday?
9. Theorized name for the *Lover* album, drawn from the *ME!* music video
10. Which song on *Midnights* is lovingly theorized to be written about Swifties?
11. "New Year's Day," the last surprise song played during the 2023 U.S. leg of the Eras Tour, had fans convinced that this re-record was coming next
12. This building in one of Swift's music videos featured rooms of various colors, styles, and designs that fans attributed to Swift's various album eras
16. According to fans, *Midnights* is rumored to be what kind of album?
17. Fans watch the ____ Building's social media accounts for clues about Swift's upcoming projects
20. Fans were originally convinced *reputation (Taylor's Version)* would be announced in what city during the Eras Tour?
21. Supposed color of theorized third sister album to *folklore* and *evermore*
23. A graffitied wall in this music video had fans spiraling about the release orders of the re-records and potential new albums
25. How many holes were in the fence?

Find 8 changes

All Too Well:
The Short Film

This lyrical masterpiece premiered following the release of *Red (Taylor's Version)* in November 2021. Making her cinematic directorial debut with the release of the short film, Swift tells the devastating and captivating story of a first love and heartbreak. Sadie Sink, Dylan O'Brien, and Taylor Swift star in this short film, which won the Grammy for Best Music Video at the 2023 Grammy Awards.

Answers on page 159.

TRIVIA

1. After its release, Taylor's debut album *Taylor Swift* sold more than a million albums in the U.S., making it certified _____.

    A. Platinum

    B. Gold

    C. Silver

    D. Bronze

2. What was Taylor's first song to reach number one on the Billboard Hot 100?

    A. "Style"

    B. "Love Story"

    C. "Karma"

    D. "We Are Never Ever Getting Back Together"

3. In March 2024, it was discovered that Taylor was related to which famous poet?

    A. Emily Dickinson

    B. Toni Morrison

    C. Walt Whitman

    D. Edgar Allan Poe

4. During an overseas leg of the Eras Tour, Taylor talked about which country where her mother Andrea spent a lot of her childhood?

    A. South Korea

    B. Singapore

    C. Ecuador

    D. Norway

5. In September 2023, in the run-up to the release of her album *1989 (Taylor's Version)*, what did Taylor ask her fans to do?

    A. Run 89 laps

    B. Plant 89 flowers

    C. Decode 89 puzzles

    D. Do 89 jumping jacks

Answers on following page.

1. **A.** Albums that sell over a million copies in the U.S. are certified platinum. And based on the reception her debut album received, Taylor was fast becoming one of the music world's brightest young stars.

2. **D.** "We Are Never Ever Getting Back Together" was the first Taylor Swift song to reach number one on the Billboard Hot 100. It was also the lead single from her 2012 album, Red.

3. **A.** Taylor is distantly related to Emily Dickinson. Specifically, they are sixth cousins, three times removed. Evidence of the connection between Taylor and Emily was discovered by Ancestry, a company which helps people trace their family lineage. And of course, this is quite appropriate because the title of Taylor's 2024 album is *The Tortured Poets Department*.

4. **B.** While performing at the National Stadium in Singapore in March of 2024, Taylor told the audience that her mother Andrea grew up in Singapore, and it was a place she'd heard about her whole life. She also said that in the past, when she went to Singapore on tour with her mother, they would drive past Andrea's childhood home.

5. **C.** She asked her fans to decode 89 word puzzles on Google to find the song titles of her 1989 vault tracks. Even though the puzzles had to be solved a whopping 33 million times to unlock the song titles, diligent Swifties cracked the code by the very next day. That's commitment!

Addagram

In addition to being scrambled, each phrase below is missing the same letter. Discover the missing letter, then unscramble the words. When you do, you'll reveal 3 Taylor Swift albums.

DING THIS

VEER ROE

A TREETOP'S DEED PORTENT TRUTH

Matching

Match each Taylor Swift music video to the celebrity who appeared in it.

1. *All Too Well: The Short Film*

2. *I Can See You*

3. *Anti-Hero*

4. *Bejeweled*

A. Mike Birbiglia

B. Laura Dern

C. Taylor Lautner

D. Sadie Sink

Answers on pages 159–160.

Place Names

Every place name mentioned in a Taylor Swift song listed is contained within the group of letters. Place names can be found in a straight line horizontally, vertically, or diagonally. They may be read either forward or backward.

ASIA

BEVERLY HILLS

BRIXTON

BROOKLYN

CAMDEN MARKET

CAROLINA

CENTENNIAL PARK

CONEY ISLAND

CORNELIA STREET

EAST SIDE

FLORIDA

GEORGIA

HACKNEY

HIGH LINE

HIGHGATE

HOLLYWOOD

INDIA

L.A.

LONDON

NEW YORK

PARIS

PENNSYLVANIA

RHODE ISLAND

SHOREDITCH

SOCAL

SOHO

ST. LOUIS

ST. TROPEZ

SUNSET AND VINE

TENNESSEE

TUPELO

UPSTATE

VEGAS

WEST SIDE

WICKLOW

WINDERMERE

E W P A R I L O D N A L S I E D O H R M M
M I N D I S M O P E N N S Y L V A N I A Z
K M C M Z A H N N W T N E W Y O N U R T X
K R O Y W E N O E D E E X D A I G R O E G
D S A V E C P S R O O L N B I S B E L K A
N I H P O T T O L E K N M N O S R N H R H
O U S R L S A E R O D P A H E E T H U A I
L O U P I A P T O T A I O N M S N S C M G
H L C D G U I R S R T F T R I Y S K A N H
I T E E T H B N I P I S E C L L N E G E L
I S T S E W K S N C U D V K H E O E E D I
T E E R T S A I L E N R O C Y K O R M M N
L A C O S S F D H I T O S T T R O P A A E
R S I Y E N O C W H R N I F G S W M S C N
I H Y L R E V E B B E V E R L Y H I L L S
I W I C K L O W P R F S I C A O A N F T B
D O O W Y L L O H I G H G A T E R D N U R
E M S A G E V D F X S X H I G H T I V P I
R A M N E D M A C T E A S T S I Z A D E X
H D N L C A H F C O N E Y I S L A N D A T
A G E V E N I V D N A T E S N U S A C O S

Matching

Match each celebrity to their alter ego in Taylor Swift's *Bad Blood* music video.

1.	Serayah	A.	Arsyn
2.	Hailee Steinfeld	B.	Frostbyte
3.	Lena Dunham	C.	Cut-Throat
4.	Ellen Pompeo	D.	Dilemma
5.	Cindy Crawford	E.	Luna
6.	Selena Gomez	F.	Catastrophe
7.	Karlie Kloss	G.	Domino
8.	Mariska Hargitay	H.	Headmistress
9.	Taylor Swift	I.	The Trinity
10.	Zendaya	J.	Justice
11.	Lily Aldridge	K.	Knockout
12.	Jessica Alba	L.	Lucky Fiori

Answers on page 160.

TTPD SCRAMBLE

Unscramble each word or phrase below to reveal a song from Taylor Swift's *The Tortured Poets Department* album.

1. SAY LINGUIST
2. COBRA LAW
3. HERSELF A MOTHER MUST
4. LOAD FIR
5. DEADBOLT HUMID IVY
6. AS THE MAD VELVETEEN'S HILL WORM
7. SOLD LONG NOON
8. LEACH THYME
9. DEAD EFFORT AS HOLLOW LIMIT
10. RIGHT FONT
11. MOLL
12. A BAA THICKENED WITHIN ROTOR
13. WAND BOD
14. EMPHATIC TURNS
15. SAFETY, OH VISITOR, YEARN SMOKY LOBBY
16. OTHER BELT
17. HARASS BOTTLE

Answers on page 160.

1989

ACROSS

1. Music video composed of footage from the 1989 World Tour
4. *1989* is which album in her discography?
6. This singer-songwriter released a cover album of *1989* in 2015
7. First single released from album
9. First name of Swift's cat featured in the *Blank Space* music video
11. Title of track 11
13. Song earning Swift the Grammy for Best Music Video
14. Taylor iconically stabs this in the *Blank Space* music video
16. Imogen Heap co-wrote this song
19. Taylor's age when she wrote *1989*
21. *1989* is the first album Taylor released that was classified entirely under this genre
24. Song written during the *1989* era for the movie *One Chance*
26. *1989*'s associated color
27. This Shawn was an opening act on the 1989 World Tour
29. Song on the album Swift admitted took her the shortest amount of time to write
30. First name of famous producer Taylor began working with during the *1989* era
32. Number of bonus tracks on the original album
33. Name of first deluxe track on original album
34. Director of the *Bad Blood* music video

DOWN

2. Animal symbol of the *1989* era
3. Each original CD contained thirteen of these
5. This vault song from *1989 (Taylor's Version)* debuted at #1 on the Billboard Hot 100
8. Joseph Kahn directed this many music videos for *1989*
10. Among other awards, *1989* won this Grammy
11. The 1989 World Tour traveled to this many countries
12. This song includes a recording of Taylor's heartbeat
15. Title of track 3
17. Number of vault songs on *1989 (Taylor's Version)*
18. First name of the love interest in the *Blank Space* music video
20. The U.S. leg of the 1989 World Tour kicked off in this city
22. Swift promoted the album with this fast food brand
23. This British rock legend appeared as a special guest during the 1989 World Tour's Nashville show
24. She played "Arsyn" in the *Bad Blood* video
25. The *Wildest Dreams* music video was inspired by this classic film
28. Number of tracks on the original version of the album
31. Number of hit singles from the album

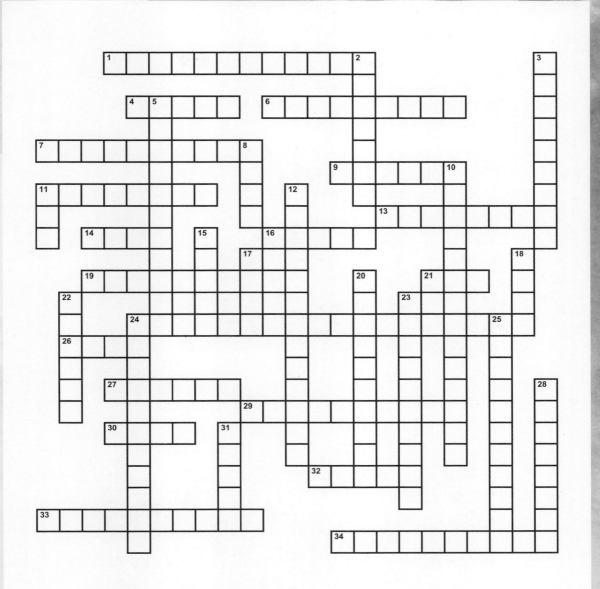

Blank Space

A smashing hit from Swift's *1989*, the *Blank Space* music video has garnered over 3.3 billion views on YouTube since its release in 2014. This video was primarily filmed at Oheka Castle in Long Island, New York, and details the chaos of a deteriorating relationship. It was directed by Joseph Kahn.

Answers on page 160.

TRIVIA

1. As a way of showing her support for her friend Ed Sheeran, Taylor appeared with him onstage at _____ in October 2013.

    A. Carnegie Hall

    B. The Hollywood Bowl

    C. The Sydney Opera House

    D. Madison Square Garden

2. It wasn't a surprise to see Taylor in September 2010 at the premiere of her friend Emma Stone's film _____.

    A. Superbad

    B. Cruella

    C. Easy A

    D. Crazy Stupid Love

3. In 2008, the EP "Beautiful Eyes" was released exclusively in which marketplace?

    A. Taylorswift.com

    B. Walmart

    C. Target

    D. Amazon

4. Among the records Taylor's Eras Tour broke is _____.

    A. Most countries visited during one tour

    B. Most costume changes ever on one stage

    C. Highest-grossing music tour ever

    D. Highest note ever sung at the London Palladium

5. In 2015, Taylor threatened to pull *1989* off which streaming service?

    A. Spotify

    B. SoundCloud

    C. Amazon Music

    D. Apple Music

Answers on following page.

1. **D.** Taylor appeared with Ed at New York City's Madison Square Garden. Together, they sang the song they'd written together, "Everything Has Changed." And just as Ed had worn an "I Heart NY" T-shirt, Taylor wore an "I Heart Ed" shirt.

2. **C.** On September 13, 2010, Taylor attended the premiere of Emma's movie Easy A. Taylor and Emma have been friends since meeting at the Young Hollywood Awards in 2008. Taylor is a loyal friend and a strong supporter of other friends' projects.

3. **B.** Although Taylor later consistently released exclusive editions through Target stores, in 2008 it was Walmart who marketed "Beautiful Eyes."

4. **C.** In December of 2023, Guinness World Records announced that Taylor's Eras Tour was the highest-grossing music tour in history, being the first to earn more than $1 billion in revenue. It broke the previous record held by Elton John's five-year farewell tour.

5. **D.** Taylor had said she would keep the album off of Apple Music. Why? Because she was upset about the music streaming service's policy of not paying royalties to artists during its free three-month trial period. But the very day after Taylor threatened to remove her album from the streamer, Apple Music reversed their policy. Taylor has always been a champion of artists' rights!

FEARLESS TOUR QUIZ

Below is a list of cities on Taylor Swift's Fearless Tour. The only thing is, they've lost all instances of A, E, I, O, U, and Y. Can you figure out the missing vowels and name each city in the list below?

1. _V_NSV_LL_

2. J_N_SB_R_

3. ST. L___S

4. _L_X_NDR__

5. J_CKS_NV_LL_

6. B_L_X_

7. L_ND_N

8. SP_K_N_

9. P_RTL_ND

10. N_MP_

11. GL_ND_L_

12. N_W BR_CKT_N

13. GR__NSB_R_

14. _SHK_SH

15. _DM_NT_N

16. _M_H_

17. T_LS_

18. CL_V_L_ND

19. R_S_M_NT

20. F_XB_R__GH

Answers on page 160.

Answers

Anti-Hero (page 4)

Addagram (page 7)

The missing letter is U.
"Teardrops on My Guitar," "Picture to Burn,"
"Should've Said No"

Matching (page 7)

1. E; 2. C; 3. F; 4. A; 5. D; 6. B

Reputation (pages 8–9)

Name the Songs (page 10)

1. "evermore" (shipwreck, barefoot in winter, rewind the tape, cabin floors); 2. "Cruel Summer" (roll dice, back of car, bar, garden gate); 3. "cardigan" (black lipstick, Peter, High Line, heels cobblestone)

Taylor Swift Scramble (page 11)

1. "Should've Said No"; 2. "Cold as You"; 3. "Our Song"; 4. "Tim McGraw"; 5. "Picture to Burn"; 6. "Teardrops on My Guitar"; 7. "Mary's Song (Oh My My My)"; 8. "A Place in This World"; 9. "Tied Together with a Smile"; 10. "The Outside"; 11. "Stay Beautiful"; 12. "A Perfectly Good Heart"

One-Word Song Titles (pages 12–13)

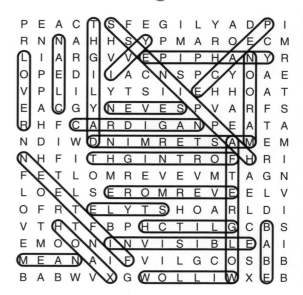

Answers

Find the Cats (page 14)

Emoji Songs (page 17)

1. "champagne problems"; 2. "Lavender Haze";
3. "Wildest Dreams"; 4. "Death by a Thousand
Cuts"; 5. "Sparks Fly"

Reputation Scramble (page 18)

1. "New Year's Day"; 2. "So It Goes..."; 3.
"Dancing with Our Hands Tied"; 4. "Getaway
Car"; 5. "This Is Why We Can't Have Nice
Things"; 6. "... Ready for It?"; 7. "End Game"; 8.
"Call It What You Want"; 9. "Delicate"; 10.
"Look What You Made Me Do"; 11. "King of My
Heart"; 12. "Gorgeous"

Word Fill-In (page 19)

Midnights (pages 20–21)

Matching (page 22)

1. C; 2. D; 3. A; 4. B

Answers

Addagram (page 22)

The missing letter is T.
"White Horse," "Love Story," "Fifteen," "You Belong with Me"

Eras Opening Acts (page 23)

Love Story (page 24)

Name the Songs (page 27)

1. "betty" (broken cobblestones, far side of the gym, in the garden, ridin' on my skateboard); 2. "King of My Heart" (Motown, broken bones, jaguars, drinking beer out of plastic cups); 3. "Begin Again" (headphones, cafe, Wednesday)

Fearless Scramble (page 28)

1. "You Belong with Me" ; 2. "Love Story"; 3. "Fearless"; 4. "White Horse"; 5. "You're Not Sorry"; 6. "Forever & Always"; 7. "The Way I Loved You"; 8. "Hey Stephen"; 9. "Breathe"; 10. "Fifteen"; 11. "The Best Day"; 12. "Mr. Perfectly Fine"; 13. "You All Over Me"

Eras Tour Quiz (page 29)

1. Versace; 2. Christian Louboutin; 3. Roberto Cavalli; 4. Etro; 5. Ashish; 6. Nicole + Felicia; 7. Alberta Ferretti; 8. Jessica Jones; 9. Zuhair Murad; 10. Oscar de la Renta

Evermore (pages 30–31)

Answers

Addagram (page 32)

The missing letter is D.
West End, Shoreditch, Camden Market,
Bond Street

Matching (page 32)

1. D; 2. C; 3. F; 4. A; 5. E; 6. B

Names in Titles (page 33)

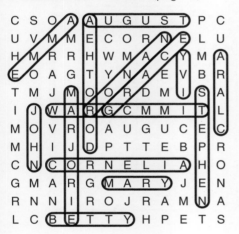

Reputation Stadium Tour Quiz (page 37)

1. Pasadena; 2. Seattle; 3. Chicago; 4. Manchester; 5. Dublin; 6. Louisville; 7. Columbus; 8. Philadelphia; 9. East Rutherford; 10. Toronto; 11. Atlanta; 12. Minneapolis; 13. Arlington; 14. Sydney; 15. Tokyo

More One-Word Titles (pages 38–39)

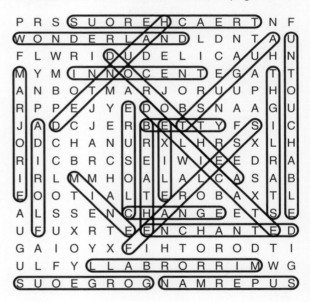

Word Fill-In (page 34)

Answers

Wildest Dreams (pages 40–41)

Fearless (pages 42–43)

Emoji Songs (page 44)

1. "Paper Rings"; 2. "Wonderland"; 3. "Long Live"; 4. "Love Story"; 5. "Cruel Summer"

Folklore Scramble (page 47)

1. "my tears ricochet"; 2. "the lakes"; 3. "invisible string"; 4. "august"; 5. "illicit affairs"; 6. "mirrorball"; 7. "the last great american dynasty"; 8. "seven"; 9. "cardigan"; 10. "this is me trying"; 11. "mad woman"; 12. "epiphany"

From the Vault (pages 48–49)

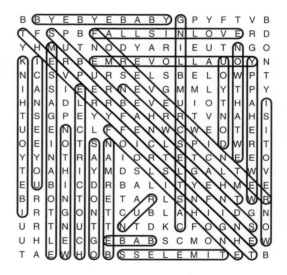

Name the Songs (page 50)

1. "the 1" (bus stop, roaring 20s, rosé flowing); 2. "You're On Your Own, Kid" (picked the petals, fireplace ashes, friendship bracelets, sprinkler splashes); 3. "peace" (ocean waves, east and west, trenches, I'm a fire)

Addagram (page 51)

The missing letter is S.
"New Romantics," "Blank Space," "Shake It Off," "Out of the Woods"

Answers

Matching (page 51)

1. C; 2. B; 3. F; 4. A; 5. E; 6. D

Speak Now (pages 52–53)

```
I N N O C E N T        H        T
O U R S   T O P C O U N T R Y A L B U M
S         T     N        L     E     I   N     A
P U R P L E   T H I R T Y T W O   T   N   E   A U
A         E     H        R        T         E   C
R   L A S T K I S S   D   J U L Y     E         K
K       C     R        I        R     H         L
S   Z E R O   D R O P S O F J U P I T E R       A
F       U     I        X        T   H           N
L   T   M     R              E N C H A N T E D   D
Y   H   B   T                E
    I   L   H    W O N D E R S T R U C K         K
    R   I   E                    E               O
    T   N   S                    V               I
    E   O                        E               F
    E   R    L           L       N               I
    N   Y    J O E Y K I N G     G               S
        Y    N           N       G               H
             S I N G A P O R E
D E A R J O H N          L
Y O U T U B E   M A K E I T H O T
        S       N E V E R G R O W U P
```

Look What You Made Me Do
(page 54)

Name the Songs (page 57)

1. "august" (bedsheets, rust on door, bottle of wine, the mall); 2. "my tears ricochet" (diamond ring, ashes, battleships sink, bury me); 3. "This Is Why We Can't Have Nice Things" (Gatsby, big parties, chandelier, axe to a mended fence)

Matching (page 58)

1. C; 2. F; 3. H; 4. K; 5. I; 6. D; 7. A; 8. E; 9. J; 10. G; 11. B

Addagram (page 59)

The missing letter is R.
folklore, reputation, Lover, Fearless

Matching (page 59)

1. C; 2. A; 3. D; 4. B

Evermore Scramble (page 60)

1. "it's time to go"; 2. "coney island"; 3. "dorothea"; 4. "evermore"; 5. "willow"; 6. "no body, no crime"; 7. "long story short"; 8. "right where you left me"; 9. "closure"; 10. "champagne problems"; 11. "cowboy like me"; 12. "tolerate it"; 13. "gold rush"

Answers

Word Fill-In (page 61)

(crossword grid with answers: LOVE, MIC, MIDNIGHTS, STORY, MINE, WRITER, POET, CRUEL, MUSIC, SUMMER, WILLOW, etc.)

Our Song (pages 62–63)

Speak Now World Tour Quiz (page 64)

1. "You Learn"; 2. "Dancing in the Dark"; 3. "Lose Yourself"; 4. "I Heard It Through the Grapevine"; 5. "Just a Dream"; 6. "God Only Knows"; 7. "Summer of '69"; 8. "Unpretty"; 9. "Drops of Jupiter"; 10. "How to Save a Life"; 11. "Baby Girl"; 12. "Wide Open Spaces"; 13. "All You Wanted"; 14. "Cry Me a River"

NYC Scramble (page 67)

1. West Village; 2. Madison Square; 3. Brooklyn; 4. Coney Island; 5. East Side; 6. West Side

Matching (page 67)

1. C; 2. A; 3. B; 4. D

Taylor Swift (pages 68–69)

(crossword grid with answers: SIXTEEN, BEAUTIFULEYES, MARYSSONG, SHOULDVESAIDNO, PICKUPTRUCK, POURINGRAIN, ELEVEN, RASCALFLATTS, THREE, MUSTANG, COUNTRYPOP, FRIEND, DEBUT, SCREENDOOR, COLDASYOU, SEVEN, TWENTYFOUR)

Answers

Find the Cats (page 70)

Taylor Swift's Influences
(pages 72–73)

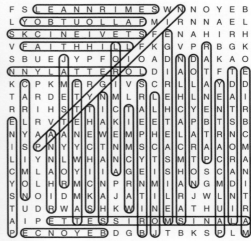

Name the Songs (page 74)

1. "Wonderland" (slept with one eye open, Cheshire Cat, green eyes, rabbit hole); 2. "Is It Over Now?" (takeout coffees, the wilt of the rose, flashing lights, blue dress on a boat); 3. "the lakes" (poets, rose grew up out of ice frozen ground, wisteria, Windermere peaks)

Celebrity Scramble (page 71)

1. RuPaul; 2. Adam Lambert; 3. Katy Perry; 4. Ryan Reynolds; 5. Chester Lockhart; 6. Billy Porter; 7. Ellen DeGeneres; 8. Laverne Cox; 9. Jesse Tyler Ferguson; 10. Adam Rippon; 11. Todrick Hall; 12. Dexter Mayfield; 13. Tan France

Starting with "The" (page 77)

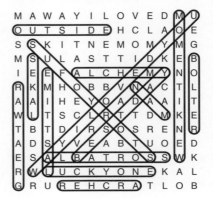

Answers

Red (pages 78–79)

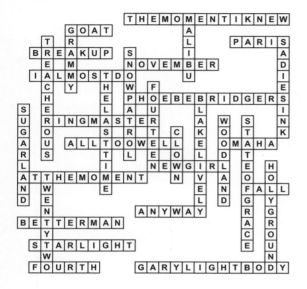

Songwriting Partners (pages 82–83)

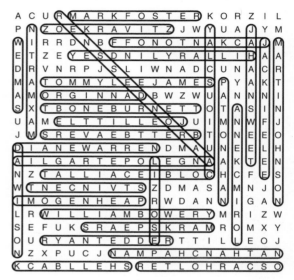

Lavender Haze (pages 80–81)

Name the Songs (page 84)

1. "New Romantics" (play my Ace, bricks they threw, busy dancing, tears of mascara); 2. "Sparks Fly" (staircase, sparks fly, house of cards, kiss me on the sidewalk); 3. "You Belong with Me" (sneakers, worn-out jeans, park bench, bleachers)

Red Tour Quiz (page 87)

1. Ed Sheeran; 2. Brett Eldredge; 3. Austin Mahone; 4. Florida Georgia Line; 5. Joel Crouse; 6. Casey James; 7. Neon Trees; 8. Guy Sebastian; 9. The Vamps; 10. Andreas Bourani

Answers

Folklore (pages 88–89)

Crossword answers including: KITTYCOMMITTEE, MYTHS, ILLICITAFFAIRS, SPARK, PSSS, HESS, EVERMORE, THELAKES, BETTYINEZJAMES, CARDIGAN, JULY, MIRRORBALL, MADWOMAN, TWO, EPIPHANY, AUGUST, GRAY, QUARANTINE, SADBEAUTIFULTRAGIC, BONIVER, PEACE, MAPLE, RHODEISLAND, CHILDHOOD

Shake It Off (page 90)

Lover Scramble (page 91)

1. "The Man"; 2. "False God"; 3. "Soon You'll Get Better"; 4. "Death by a Thousand Cuts"; 5. "Afterglow"; 6. "Cruel Summer"; 7. "The Archer"; 8. "You Need to Calm Down"; 9. "Cornelia Street"; 10. "Paper Rings"; 11. "It's Nice to Have a Friend"; 12. "London Boy"; 13. "I Think He Knows"; 14. "Miss Americana & the Heartbreak Prince"

Oh That Vocabulary! (pages 92–93)

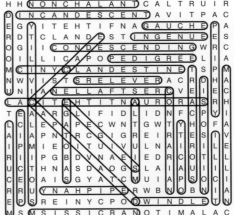

Matching (page 94)

1. C; 2. E; 3. D; 4. B; 5. A

Addagram (page 94)

The missing letter is D.
"End Game," "New Year's Day," "Delicate," "... Ready for It?"

Answers

Begin Again (page 97)

Recording Studios (pages 98–99)

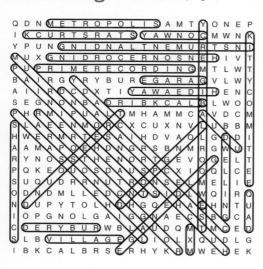

Word Fill-In (page 101)

			S	H	A	K	E				
	S			L			P				
	I		T		B	L	O	O	D		
	N		R		U		P				T
	G	R	A	M	M	Y					I
O			C								T
F	O	L	K		V		B				L
O					O		A	I	N	D	I	E
V					I		C				
E					C						
R	E	L	E	A	S	E					

Bejeweled (pages 102–103)

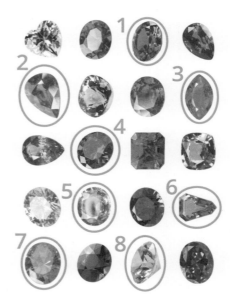

Speak Now Scramble (page 100)

1. "The Story of Us"; 2. "Mean"; 3. "Dear John"; 4. "Mine"; 5. "Haunted"; 6. "Enchanted"; 7. "Sparks Fly"; 8. "Better than Revenge"; 9. "Back to December"; 10. "Never Grow Up"; 11. "Last Kiss"; 12. "Long Live"; 13. "Speak Now"; 14. "Superman"; 15. "Castles Crumbling"

Name the Songs (page 104)

1. "Enchanted" (2 AM, passing notes, blushing); 2. "Red" (blue, solve a crossword, dead end street, dark gray); 3. "Delicate" (phone lights up my nightstand, make me a drink, footsteps on the stairs, third floor)

Answers

Red Scramble (page 107)

1. "Treacherous"; 2. "I Knew You Were Trouble.";
3. "Holy Ground"; 4. "The Last Time"; 5. "State of Grace"; 6. "We Are Never Ever Getting Back Together"; 7. "Sad Beautiful Tragic"; 8. "The Lucky One"; 9. "Begin Again"; 10. "I Almost Do";
11. "Everything Has Changed"; 12. "Starlight";
13. "The Very First Night"; 14. "Come Back... Be Here"; 15. "Better Man"

Find the Cats (page 111)

Lover (pages 108–109)

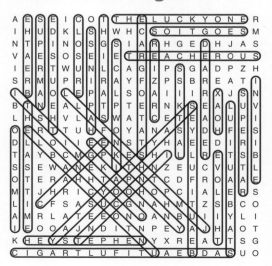

Addagram (page 110)

The missing letter is Y.
"Labyrinth," "The Alchemy," "coney island," "The Story of Us," "epiphany," "cowboy like me," "this is me trying," "Daylight," "no body, no crime," "Guilty as Sin?"

Underrated Songs (pages 112–113)

Answers

Name the Songs (page 114)

1. "I Think He Knows" (16th Avenue, hand on my thigh, skipping, architect); 2. "right where you left me" (glass shattered, at the restaurant, pages turn, matches burn); 3. "Mastermind" (checkmate, planets aligned, liquor in our cocktails, dominoes cascaded)

Emoji Songs (page 117)

1. "Our Song"; 2. "Starlight"; 3. "the last great american dynasty"; 4. "Look What You Made Me Do"; 5. "Tied Together with a Smile"; 6. "You Need to Calm Down"

1989 Scramble (page 118)

1. "Bad Blood"; 2. "How You Get the Girl"; 3. "This Love"; 4. "I Know Places"; 5. "Wildest Dreams"; 6. "Clean"; 7. "Welcome to New York"; 8. "All You Had to Do Was Stay"; 9. "Blank Space"; 10. "Shake It Off"; 11. "Out of the Woods"; 12. "New Romantics"; 13. "Sweeter than Fiction"; 14. "Now That We Don't Talk"; 15. "Suburban Legends"

Word Fill-In (page 119)

Eras Tour (pages 120–121)

I Can See You (page 122)

Midnights Scramble (page 125)

1. "Labyrinth"; 2. "Paris"; 3. "Dear Reader"; 4. "Question... ?"; 5. "Hits Different"; 6. "Bigger Than the Whole Sky"; 7. "Anti-Hero"; 8. "Lavender Haze"; 9. "Mastermind"; 10. "Midnight Rain"; 11. "Would've, Could've, Should've"; 12. "You're On Your Own, Kid"; 13. "Karma"; 14. "Maroon"; 15. "Snow on the Beach"; 16. "Sweet Nothing"

Answers

Colorful Songs (pages 126–127)

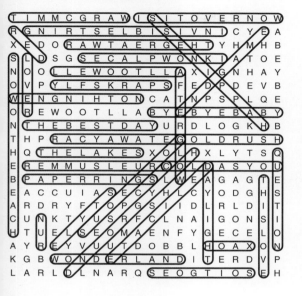

Fan Theories (pages 130–131)

1989 World Tour Quiz (page 128)

1. "Welcome to New York"; 2. "New Romantics"; 3. "Blank Space"; 4. "I Knew You Were Trouble."; 5. "I Wish You Would"; 6. "How You Get the Girl"; 7. "I Know Places"; 8. "All You Had to Do Was Stay"; 9. "You Are in Love"; 10. "Clean"; 11. "Love Story"; 12. "Style"; 13. "This Love"; 14. "Bad Blood"; 15. "We Are Never Ever Getting Back Together"; 16. "Enchanted"/"Wildest Dreams"; 17. "Out of the Woods"; 18. "Shake It Off"

Name the Songs (page 129)

1. "High Infidelity" (records, April 29th, constellations, picket fence); 2. "Karma" (queen, acrobat, cat, pennies); 3. "It's Nice to Have a Friend" (video games, sidewalk chalk, church bells, sleeping in tents)

All Too Well: The Short Film (page 132)

Addagram (page 135)

The missing letter is M.
Midnights, evermore, The Tortured Poets Department

Answers

Matching (page 135)

1. D; 2. C; 3. A; 4. B

Place Names (pages 136–137)

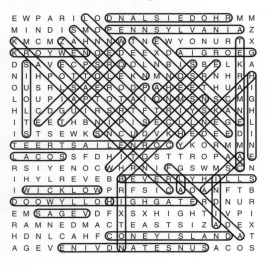

Matching (page 138)

1. D; 2. I; 3. L; 4. E; 5. H; 6. A; 7. K; 8. J; 9. F; 10. C; 11. B; 12. G

TTPD Scramble (page 139)

1. "Guilty as Sin?"; 2. "Clara Bow"; 3. "Fresh Out the Slammer"; 4. "Florida!!!"; 5. "But Daddy I Love Him"; 6. "The Smallest Man Who Ever Lived"; 7. "So Long, London"; 8. "The Alchemy"; 9. "Who's Afraid of Little Old Me?"; 10. "Fortnight"; 11. "Loml"; 12. "I Can Do It with a Broken Heart"; 13. "Down Bad"; 14. "The Manuscript"; 15. "My Boy Only Breaks His Favorite Toys"; 16. "The Bolter"; 17. "The Albatross"

1989 (pages 140–141)

Blank Space (page 142)

Fearless Tour Quiz (page 145)

1. Evansville; 2. Jonesboro; 3. St. Louis; 4. Alexandria; 5. Jacksonville; 6. Biloxi; 7. London; 8. Spokane; 9. Portland; 10. Nampa; 11. Glendale; 12. New Brockton; 13. Greensboro; 14. Oshkosh; 15. Edmonton; 16. Omaha; 17. Tulsa; 18. Cleveland; 19. Rosemont; 20. Foxborough